The Power of

ACCIDENTAL
INCREASE

Why some people create more by accident

than others do by purpose...

by

Steven M. Sisler

PRESS

A Division of the Diogenes Consortium

SANFORD • FLORIDA

Published by DC Press
2445 River Tree Circle
Sanford, FL 32771
http://www.focusonethics.com

    For orders other than individual consumers, DC Press grants discounts on purchases of 10 or more copies of single titles for bulk use, special markets, or premium use. For further details, contact:
    Special Sales — DC Press
    2445 River Tree Circle, Sanford, FL 32771
    TEL: 866-602-1476

Book set in: Adobe Jensen Pro
Cover Design and Composition by Jonathan Pennell

Library of Congress Catalog Number:
  Sisler. Steven M.
The Power of Accidental Increase: Why some people create more by accident than others do by purpose...
  ISBN: 978-1-932021-57-4

First DC Press Edition
10 9 8 7 6 5 4 3 2 1
Printed in the United States of America

Dedicated to my dear wife of 25 years and children who have always believed in me since the beginning... I am amazed at how you are all turning out in life. My undying hope is that you will all make a significant dent in the earth.

Honey; your depth of love and commitment is not human.

Contents

Acknowledgements

Thank you Seth Andreson and Kevin Rizo for your help and insights; your love for me and what I am doing is felt.

Forword

I'VE BEEN GIVEN THE OPPORTUNITY to introduce a person who has gone through a personal transformation. When I first spoke to Steve, he was the owner of Dreamkote Corporation, a small custom painting firm located on the South Shore of Massachusetts. I'm a behavioral analyst. I work with organizations to help them hire individuals who will be successful and productive in their jobs. I also work with individuals to determine their ideal occupation.

Steve completed a behavioral assessment at the insistence of a relative. After evaluating the results of the survey, it was very clear he was not reaching his fullest potential. I said; "you are not a painter nor are you a businessman for that matter... When I matched your scores up against the 25,000 people in our database, 90% were people on a mission. What's yours?"

Steve's reply was; "I always wanted to be a leader and make a difference in the lives of others. There is a lot of potential within people and I think I can help. Up until now, I wasn't really sure about where I was going, but you confirmed it. How do I get started?" Steve became an apprentice with my company and after 6 months of hard work he was ready to go out on his own and make the difference he knew he could.

Steve's style is best described as "arresting." People who know him have come to recognize his "in your face," "cut to the chase" manner of speaking. They either love it or they run for the hills. If it's not your style, it won't be long before you begin to feel it. But for those who recognize its worth, his advice is invaluable. Steve is an experience you won't soon forget. Steve doesn't have all the answers; no one really does. He will however share what he has learned through his personal experiences and that which he has gleaned from others – and he'll do it directly and pointedly… not wasting a minute's time.

I expect that Steve Sisler will become one of the nation's leading authorities in understanding and stimulating the human potential. His gift to penetrate into the human potential and his ability to inspire and channel people into new levels of achievement will make room for him.

So fasten your seat belt and enjoy the ride.

—**Grant Mazmanian, CPVA CPBA**
President, Pinnacle Group International, Inc.

Preface

"How many a man has dated a new era in his life from the reading of a book! The book exists for us, perchance, that will explain our miracles and reveal new ones. The at present unutterable things we may find somewhere uttered."

—Henry David Thoreau

THIS PUBLICATION HAS BEEN MORE ACCIDENTAL than purposeful in its creation. I no more would have imagined that I would be writing a book than I would have imagined being an astronaut juggling plates. While this is true, I also tend to run headlong into the woods blindfolded as a default attempt to find purpose and meaning in life. Yes, I admit it! It is in these precarious moments that I actually become crazy enough to believe that even I might have reason to exist in this world. And so…I am writing.

Let me give you a bird's eye view of my personal journey. Some time ago, I was diagnosed with severe ADHD. As an explanation for all of you who do not suffer from this, I call it the "Hyper Kinetic Freak Show Disorder." (HKFSD) My life seemed to evolve out of a series of freak accidents (including my birth), happening one after another without any noticeable meaning or purpose. For me, this was like being daily drug through a brush heap backwards. My first decade of school, was not only bad for me, it was unimaginatively evil. I was harassed, picked on or maimed every day for the better (or worse) part of these ten years. My most prominent memory was being stripped down to my underwear and locked in a gym locker by my fellow classmates. This locker was about six inches wide and latched with a combination lock.

There I was in seventh grade, left for dead. I can still feel the utter humiliation as I type these words now. Everyone in the class seemed to be in on the joke, so asking for help was out of the question. I was eventually discovered and released to my own demise. I write "my own demise" because later that day, eleven kids decided it was necessary to totally destroy what dignity I had left by attacking me in front of everyone and leaving me completely unconscious in the school yard (this explains a lot to those who've ever met me). I awoke to the worst-case scenario: school had ended and I was alone without a bus ride. Walking home meant the insurmountable task of negotiating every bully from there to the house, which was probably about a four-mile walk (barefoot, in the snow, uphill both ways, etc.) Obviously I made it.

Have you ever noticed that the devil doesn't fight fair? For example, my seventh grade reading teacher, Mr. Eagan picked me up by the hair and kicked me in the behind in front of my entire class. I was then promptly placed in a different class-the one that met in the library balcony. My new class consisted of children who suffered from Downs Syndrome. The faculty thought I might be mildly retarded. They told my parents, "We just want Steven to know he actually does have friends." What the faculty didn't know was that I did have some very close friends...they just happened to be invisible. I spoke with them and played with them every day until I was in eighth grade. I called them *"Flea-ah-doo-ah, Comen* and *Dee-ah."* They were my three best friends in the whole (invisible) world. They loved me for who I was — skinny, loud, obnoxious, foolish and highly trusting. I have since learned the proverb of Solomon, "A fools mouth invites a beating...," and now realize why some things happened as they did.

A dear friend once told me I was a late bloomer; boy was he right! As I reflect on every endeavor I have ever attempted to engage in, I can see now that although I began as buckshot, I have over the years increasingly become a bullet — and this by total accident on my part. I say accident because I never planned it. Not only did I not plan it, I never imagined it. I have a way of seeing about ten inches ahead of myself and so the idea of having to plan things always makes my hair hurt. As anonymous once said,

"Sometimes you just have to jump off and build your wings on the way down."

I remember painstakingly taping the broken pieces of a dismembered pen to my left arm under my sleeve — there was a bright brass spring and the little inner workings of the rear assembly. I remember thinking that I was bionic. I would entertain the idea of revealing my bionic prowess to those unfortunate bullies when the time was right, only the right time never came. The clock moved forward and my invisible friends slowly vanished into the past as I entered high school and then junior college. In tenth grade, my family moved. I spent the last two years of high school in another state and there gloried in my secret identity. It was very good for me. I was able to let bygones be bygones, but I also learned a new technique: the art of entertaining my adversaries. One day, I actually decided to bite a live catfish in half during my history class for four dollars and fifty cents. I won the money and more importantly, a new nickname-Catfish. This became my new identity. Not bad, from flounder to Catfish. It was a step in the right direction anyway, especially when combined with my new bodybuilding efforts.

"I have chosen you out of the furnace of affliction..." **Isaiah 48:10**

You might ask me why I'm writing all this? Because I want you to know who is writing it. I want you to understand where I am coming from. I want you to love me for who I am. I'm just another person who has a history of failures as well as some successes, of pain and pleasure, lucid moments of stupidity and several bright ideas. Let me be clear; I do not define success by monetary increase although they often tend to go hand in hand. Success is contentment and joy no matter the circumstances, a rare find indeed.

This is what I've learned, what I've discovered by complete accident, and what I willingly share with you.

—Steve Sisler

1

"CQ" The Character Quotient

The Power of Character

"If most of us are ashamed of shabby clothes and shoddy furniture, let us be more ashamed of shabby ideas and shoddy philosophies... It would be a sad situation if the wrapper were better than the meat wrapped inside it."

— ALBERT EINSTEIN

Character Leads

If I could sum it up in a nutshell, I'd tell you that character leads because it leads to greatness. I say this because the true value of anything is always *internal* not *external*. This is why we paint particleboard and varnish oak. We paint to conceal. We varnish because we appreciate the beauty as well as the flaws of great wood and we don't try to hide it. It's amazing how the imperfections become almost coveted within certain types of trees and more often than not, they draw attention to the artisan that considers them. Character

"The true value of anything is always internal not external. This is why we paint particleboard and varnish oak."

is much like a fine wood grain; its beauty is timeless, and when it's allowed to mature, its value increases.

While imperfections can be visually pleasing, the deeper process of varnishing is what provides lasting protection and allows for a lifetime of enjoyment. Some of the most expensive woods have been found submerged in America's hidden waterways for upwards of two hundred years. These sunken logs are valuable because they were hewn from *virgin*[1] forests. These forests were hundreds if not thousands of years old and the wood proves it. This leads to a very tight and dense grain, which from a furniture's point of view gives you a very dense and stable product. Now here's the rub; that which others may see as marred or even worthy of the Dump heap, many see as precious, fine and expensive. Painting such a valuable piece would be unimaginable to most.

We tend to cover and mask unauthentic or unappreciated merchandise in this culture; this is true with furniture, it's true with people. In terms of furniture, the beauty and stability of fine wood becomes necessary when faced with a great deal of activity and interaction. Humans, much like furniture, are extremely interactive and potentially fragile. We are sat on, scratched, nicked, tipped over and pushed around all the time. When our character is strong, our stability and longevity becomes much more dependable. And like people, every tree is a product of its environment; whether by fire or drought, each and every tree tells a story.

Scientists can detect drought patterns within moisture sensitive trees such as the *Ponderosa pine* and the *Douglas fir* because their rings can reflect stream flow within any given year. We too can reflect personal droughts within our own lives, and will capture within our cores the pains as well as the joys just like the rings of a tree. These layers build over time to reflect our ever-changing environment whether good or bad and will in the early stages

---

1 A type of forest that has attained great age and so exhibits unique biological features.

of adulthood begin the solidification of our world view. I had a tree in my backyard that from all outside appearances seemed fine, but within its center was rotten through and through.

Not until a windstorm blew the tree over did I know the depth of its rottenness. Conversely, I've noticed people that look imperfect on the outside, but have been though a process of "*environmental difficulty*" in the hands of the creator and as a result, their inside is gold. Each time I see these people or read about them, their stories put me through the washing machine and turn my world upside down. Paul Potts,[2] 2007 winner of Britain's Got Talent is a prime example of this. Though a simple carphone salesman for years, one moment changed his life forever when with a literal flip of a coin he decided to audition for the show. His character completes the story. Painting such an exquisite piece I would think unimaginable — but that's not the media's stance, they have already begun the makeover. Let's hope they don't corrupt his insides as well.

Attitudes and the Character Base

Before we indulge further the ideas of character, I want to build you a framework of where the modern ideas surrounding our attitudes and values come from. As we begin to uncover the roots of character, I want to inform you at the outset that values, character, attitudes and beliefs are all *synonymous* in their root form—they are in the same family. When I use these terms, for the most part, they will be interchangeable. To help us understand this framework, we must first take a brief look at a few people who did vital work on these subjects. I will begin with German Philosopher and Psychologist Eduard Spranger,[3] who earned his Ph.D. at the University of Berlin in 1909. In his famous book, 'Types of Men'—*Die Labensformen*-1914, Spranger detailed six types of Values all people posess.

Each persons' Values and Behavior can be *measured* and *classified* in specific areas called Values and actions. Our actions result from our Values

---

2 *Paul Potts*: (born 13 October 1970) is a British tenor who won the first series of TV's Britain's Got Talent in 2007, singing an operatic aria, "Nessun Dorma" from Puccini's Turandot. Potts was a manager at Car phone Warehouse who also performed in amateur opera from 1999 to 2003.

3 Spranger's contribution to personality theory, in his book Types of Men (Lebensformen; Halle (Saale): Niemeyer, 1914; translation by P. J. W. Pigors; New York: G. E. Stechert Company, 1928).

or who *we are on the inside*. Spranger's Values (Motivators on the inside) consisted of six differing categories, which he outlined as *Theoretical, Economic, Aesthetic, Social, Political* and *Religious*. Although these Values don't necessarily display themselves through body language, they are always the driving force ultimately responsible for why we do the things we do. In other words, when we are doing the things we value like supporting a cause we believe in, the drive to do so comes from the *inside* — the Value Base. According to Spranger, every emotional desire we have falls under one of these six Values.

Spranger believed that a person's Values were *predetermined* and that as one gets older, one ultimately becomes what one already is. Just like the tree I alluded to earlier, it may undergo different changes, but all in all, it is the same seed. Gordon Willard Allport,[4] a personality psychologist who spent the better part of his distinguished career as a professor at Harvard University, along with the help of P.E. Vernon and G. Lindzey, re-developed the study of Values in 1931. Allport, Vernon and Lindzey's work produced an assessment tool based on Spranger's six Values. Allport differed from Spranger in that he (Allport) believed that the "self" (proprium) was motivated by *environmental* and *social* elements (External stimuli) as we discussed earlier, as opposed to just a hard wiring that we happen to be born with.

Like Allport, I believe we are about 70%-80% products of our environment and influences brought upon us by those we admire, value and respect (Behaviorally). The rest is DNA (Hard wiring) and a few mystery elements. In other words, most of what we have become has been brought about by our surroundings between the ages of 1 and 8. These may include our parents, siblings and environmental factors such as living conditions, Geographic's, neighbors, and anything else that can affect a child on the inside including the family pet. Although we have certain "bents" from the beginning, the environment will have a tremendous affect on how we turn out as adults.

As a parent, we should take these ideas seriously and endeavor to be the best all around influence we can possibly be. Leaving society to do the

---

4 *Gordon Willard Allport* (November 11, 1897 — October 9, 1967) was an American psychologist. Allport was one of the first psychologists to focus on the study of the personality, and is often referred to as one of the founding figures of personality psychology. He rejected both a psychoanalytic approach to personality, which he thought often went too deep, and a behavioral approach, which he thought often did not go deep enough.

job is paramount to child abuse in my humble opinion. Who better to do the job than the ones who love the child most? I personally hold to the idea that although harmful environments exist around us, ultimately it is the positive influences that mark us the most.

Negative influences tend to be "rejected" by our natural self even though we may not fully comprehend their place in our lives at the time. I'm not saying that negative elements will not affect our behavior because they really do and sometimes in a big way. I am saying that *ultimately*, we are defined not by the bad, but by the good. For example, many of us remember a single teacher in our life who made us feel capable and important. This memory will tend to stand out among the ugly ones for sure.

Trait Theory

Most psychologists accept this understanding of the why of our *actions* today. If you have ever been praised for a job well done, you understand the spiritual lifting process that one receives as compensation. On the other hand, if you have ever been scolded for performing poorly, you understand the wet blanket feeling of depression that dawns like a misty grey morning in the mind of your poor unfortunate soul. I don't know anyone who likes being treated that way, including myself!

Gordon Allport was considered a trait theorist because he believed that every person had a small number of *specific* traits that predominated in his or her personality as a whole-*you may see these in your children if you have been fortunate enough to have them*. He specifically named these "Central Traits." While these Central Traits share in the make-up of personality, he also argued that occasionally *one* of them becomes an overriding force. He called this a "*Cardinal Trait.*" Both the central traits and the occasional cardinal trait according to Allport are environmentally, as opposed to genetically predisposed although behaviors appear more predetermined than values.[5]

I have three children and they are all different. My oldest daughter's Cardinal Trait is a quiet/sensitive demeanor. My middle son is argumentative and logic based while my youngest is explosive, angry and highly theo-

---

5 There is always an element of DNA that hard wires a person.

retically minded. They all have the same parents and have been disciplined using the same standard. The environment has always been the same within the home and we have always loved and cherished each one with respect and equal concern and yet the stark differences between them seem profound. Much of this seems to be their *hard wiring* from birth. My daughter was originally extremely stubborn, but over time has changed dramatically. The stubborn streak may have been changed by our consistent redirecting it, otherwise we must chalk it up as another mystery.

As a child matures through his/her exposure to differing social and environmental elements, specific behaviors and Values both external and internal in nature become a part of the individual's character. These in turn develop into beliefs. In other words, they become so much a part of that person that they no longer require whatever it was that caused them to develop — they (Values/Behavior) now run on their own power.

This is why our Values are very difficult to change later in life (This does not mean that certain events won't "*adjust*" these values, it's just far more difficult as we get older to change them on demand). Once these core Values are formed, like pulling a tree out of the ground it will be very hard to change them (Even saplings seem impossible to pull out at times).

This does not mean that our attitudes need to be changed, it means that they are *difficult* to change if we for some reason decide that our attitudes need adjusting. Many times traumatic events such as a divorce, spiritual experience, major move, winning the lottery or the loss of a child can effect these values.

Measuring Values

The values of an individual can be measured through a simple 10-minute questionnaire called a P.I.A.V. Report. The initials are denoted as *Personal Interests, Attitudes* and *Values*. In this questionnaire, the person is asked to answer twelve questions designed to reflect six foundational attitudes discovered and developed over the last century by individuals like Spranger and Allport. There are also many other individuals making significant contributions in the area of the original six attitudes. One such person is *Bill*

Bonnstetter,[1] president and CEO of Target Training International, Ltd. He is considered by some to be the modern leader in human resource development. Again, the person is asked to answer a series of questions by using the six multiple-choice answers provided.

The person answers by putting them in the order of importance, "*one*" being the most important and "*six*" being the least important. This method determines what each individual tends to value and will produce a graph outlining where each person stands in their value base and what two or three top attitudes are driving them.

The power of this report becomes remarkable in the hands of a seasoned expert. 20 minutes into the debrief, you will enter a different stratosphere that I call "*Crazy Talk*."[2] Character, gifting and IQ are all variables that can be gathered from such a report when an *expert* in Values Analysis is reading the results. Now, I must admit, I used to be a bit dazed and confused when people asked me, "*Steve, what should I do with my life?*" I even asked that question a time or two myself.

Want to go from carphone salesman to phenom? This report puts the Uranium in Nuclear and will lend you the guidance you need to help sort things out... and it's Crazy Talk!

The Four Quadrants

The four quadrants are derived from my 20 years of study on the human soul. Observable indicators are those actions, which can be perceived by others readily through body language, voice tone, mannerisms, etc. The behavioral elements, what we see, represent the direct reflection of the Values or Character Base in many ways. Although our Values remain at times undetected, our actions will reveal the inner value

"Although our Values remain at times undetected, our actions will reveal the inner value system by the things that those actions produce.

---

1 *Bill Bonnstetter*: founder of Target Training International, Ltd. (TTI) has staged a 20-year innovation and development of the DISC Language.
2 *Crazy Talk*: when what is being said surpasses your cranial ball of mishmash.

system by the things that those actions produce. To give you an example, an action that produces self-gratification at the expense of someone else will expose a selfish attitude.

For the past 10 years or so, I have called the four quadrants, "*The 4 pillars of your life*" and for good reason. The four quadrants become paramount to *Accidental Increase* for all who have settled them within their own heart (we will discuss the heart in chapter five). The four quadrants cover the four things that not only hold your life together, but also are the very foundation on which it rests. They are the *Creed*, the *Character*, the *Conduct* and the *Convictions* that we live by.

The Creed Base

Your creed is any system of beliefs, principles, or strong opinions derived from the environmental *quantum foam* you were raised in. "*Quantum foam*" is a phrase that I stole from quantum Physicist Brian Greene several years ago.[3] It means simply this — *the smaller you travel towards the atomic level, the weirder things get*. I'll go out on a limb and say we all have "weird" somewhere in the family tree, and most of us have "weird" within our own immediate family!

Our creed is what we believe — period. And although we have not fully developed what we believe about let's say C, our ultimate ideas about C will be consequent upon what we *think we know* about A and B. You see, what we *already* (Presently) believe will have a tremendous impact on what we *will* (Future) believe about the yet undiscovered. This is why most of us will carry on with the belief system adhered to during our formation years (1-11).

I have a friend who was the owner of a small painting company (He has since endeavored to do something else). He took a chance on a kid we'll call Bill[4] because he noticed that Bill had good eye/hand coordination and skill. Being a fine judge of talent, within a year or so, Bill rose to the heights of painting success. Bill, the adept employee, began to manage his boss's

---

3 *The Elegant Universe*: Vintage Books, Random House, Inc. NY, New York; Brian R. Greene, Copyright 1999, 2003.
4 This is a fictitious name. I used it in order to protect this poor soul.

painting business. Bill was so talented that the boss began to leave his crew and jobs in Bill's capable hands.

One day, the boss showed up on a job that Bill was managing, and he was so happy that he put his arm around Bill and said, "Bill, you are my strong workhorse!" To the boss's bewilderment, Bill began to get very angry and red in the face. Bill dropped his paint bucket and said, "I ain't nobodies' nothin'!" and walked off. Bill's boss was the startled victim of Bill's Quantum Foam run amuck. Bill's creed, character and conduct got in the way of a great opportunity for him to succeed.

For the most part, all of our current actions are stemming from our personal creeds. You might say, "I don't believe in anything." Well then, if that is the case, you will by default believe nothing (Wow Steve, that's ingenious!). You have to understand this concept; the fact is this, believing in *nothing* will determine how you act just as much as believing in *something* will. People with a strong creed will tend towards *Accidental Increase* much faster than those who *never* become resolute in their beliefs.

You may say, "I am resolute in the fact that I do not believe anything!" I say well, you are resolute then. This is not about *believing* in something or *not believing* in something, it's about landing your plane. It's when we act unstable and cannot come to a conclusion about a matter that keeps us from success and *Accidental Increase*. Even the Christ says in John's Revelation, "*I would rather you become either hot or cold, but don't be lukewarm!*"[5]   In other words, be either Billy Graham or Attila the Hun, but don't be a Politician.

In order to sum up this section, you must ask yourself a few very important questions beginning with, "What are my beliefs?" Do you have any? You should. You should be able to tell me right now without hesitation exactly what you believe and why. What do you believe about people in general? About life? Why are you here and where are you going? The answers to these very important questions and why you believe them will have a huge impact on where you go from here. And since I'm at it, let me say this, you will never have all the answers. Believing takes faith my friend, knowledge doesn't. *Faith* will always take you farther than *facts* ever will — never forget it.

---

5 John's Crazy Revelation 3:16

The Character Base

Character is representative of what we *are* and will ultimately be the all-encompassing element of this entire section. What we *are* determines what we *believe* just like we discussed in the creed section. This is your wood grain. If you believe in chivalry and courtesy, your actions will be displayed by holding the door open for people and by saying please and thank you. Your observable manners are a product of your beliefs about them. If you believe it to be cold outside, you will put on a jacket.

> Part of *Accidental Increase* is acting in line with your beliefs."

If your parents or guardian found these traits important, then they may have put pressure on you to display them. If you have personally bought into the idea, you will not have much trouble with the behavioral display except for minor moments of forgetfulness. Character therefore, is definitely one of the most powerful ingredients for *Accidental Increase*. This is the ability to be the same person in private as you are in public. Part of *Accidental Increase* is being completely true to whom you are all the time. No gaps. Characteristically predictable. What I'm saying is that those who know you well can predict what you would do in any given situation based upon their knowledge of your personal tree rings.

Take *integrity* for instance, it speaks very loudly even in today's society. If you understand the word integrity, you will know that it comes from the word *integer*. Integer means untouched, whole, or entire. You are a whole person if you display integrity. You are in an *unbroken* condition. This means you are the same on Sunday afternoon as you are on Friday night. The condition of your soul remains the same; this is not about *perfection*, it's about *consistency*. If you break the condition, you make it right as soon as you become aware of the misstep and you do it without argument. People with high integrity tend to create *Accidental Increase* because their consistency pays off over time. Inconsistency *never* produces a great result.

You can't be wishy-washy in what you believe and you can't be wishy-washy in who you are if you want to increase. In the Bible, James[6] (Jesus' half

---

6 James 1:1-8

brother) says that a double-minded man is unstable in *everything* he does; he should not expect to receive anything from God because he lives as though tossed around by the waves of the sea — *he cannot land his plane*. Integrity and consistency go hand in hand. Integrity and increase go hand in hand as well.

There's a very interesting story found in the Genesis narrative in the Old Testament of the Bible. In the 20th chapter, Abraham moves to the region of the Negev and while there, happens to stay in this place called Gerar for a while and because he feared for his life, he claimed his wife to be his sister. She was apparently pretty cute to say the least! Because of this, Abimelech, the king of Gerar, took her into his harem to become one of his prized possessions believing her to be available for his taking.

This is when all hell breaks loose. Apparently, God appeared to Abimelech in a dream and said that he was as good as dead for taking another man's wife! This sets about a fire storm of monumental proportions within the heart of the king and so he pleads for his life within the dream (Probably a smart move). This is where it gets interesting; Abimelech tells God that he acted out of the integrity (*Integer*) of his heart when he took Abraham's wife. One translation reads, "*a clear conscience.*" This is when Abimelech makes the case to God for acting with *pure* intentions.

While still within the dream, God says to Abimelech; "I know, that is why *I kept you from touching her.*" This is an amazing story because of what is actually taking place within the dynamics of integrity and character as it plays out in the life of this obscure king. Did you catch it? Did you catch what happened here? Let me put it another way; Solomon says in one of his proverbs that the integrity of the upright actually becomes their guide.[7] When you operate out of a pure conscience or out of integrity, you avoid pitfalls just like Abimelech did.

The king avoided disaster for the simple reason that he *meant well* when he took Abraham's wife (Remember, he didn't know she was married). He acted on reasonable grounds considering what he *believed* to be *true* and not in a way that was *against* Abraham. He was simply doing what kings do, not stealing another man's wife — and this became his ultimate salvation.

---

7 Proverbs 11:3

Another interesting thing about this story is found when the king forces Abraham to explain his actions. Abraham tells the king that he said to himself; "*...there is surely no fear of God in this place.*" What an assumption! Can you believe that? It appears that Abimelech had more character than Abraham did - what a dreadful misjudgment! You will find in this world that some people are better by *nature* than others are by *grace*. Assumption is lifes *lowest* level of knowledge and sadly, most folks begin there when assessing most situations because they are too lazy to look into it. Jesus said, "*Never judge by outward appearances. Make righteous judgments.*"[8] You should do the same from now on.

The Conduct Base

Conduct is simply what we *do*. Our *conduct* serves as a medium for conveying or *transmitting* our Values from the hidden *quantum* arena of belief to public life where others can see them. This is about translating or *transferring* inner beliefs and ideas into outward actions and indicators that can be observed by others. Just as some forms of metal can conduct heat by transmitting it to another material, our beliefs are also transmitted to other people through our conduct or actions.

These actions will determine our success rate with profound accuracy. Part of *Accidental Increase* is acting in line with your beliefs. Sadly, many people will believe one thing and under pressure act contrary to it. If you read the label of most any household cleaner, you will find an interesting note within its directions for use; "It is a violation of *federal law* to use this product in a manner that is inconsistent with its labeling." Wow!

Although we are all worth far more than a bottle of Windex®,[9] many of us fail to take *our* labeling seriously. Living consistent with your confession will always take you farther than talking out of both sides of your mouth ever will. It's a terrible portrait we paint when we *claim* one thing and *live* another. How often we violate a *fundamental law* when we preach standards we can't live up to. When I was younger I recall hearing people say about others, "*they practice what they preach.*" I have since altered that statement to

---

8 John 7:24
9 A chemical agent used for cleaning glass and assaulting ants from time to time.

fit within a paradigm that works; *only preach what you already practice and leave everything else alone and you won't be wasting your time cleaning dung off your face.* I suppose I should be thankful for not ending up in prison because I violated a federal law when spraying ants with Windex® when I was a kid.

Consistency in conduct is huge when it comes to success. It creates an assumed reliability that others will learn to predetermine and count on. There's nothing worse than being away and wondering what an important individual is doing in your absence. The more we can relax when we think of those who work for us, the better. This also goes for those we are dating, married to, etc.

Reliability is one of the keys to *Accidental Increase* if you haven't started to figure this out. When what we do and what we say become synonymous, we create a synergy that becomes unstoppable. Make sure your actions speak in direct line with your words especially in front of your kids because they don't do what you say, they do what you do; never forget it.

You will find that most everyone respects this behavior in people regardless of the belief system they hold. Conveying your interior beliefs with your exterior self allows others to know who you *really* are. One of the reasons why American marriages end in divorce to the tune of 37% today[10] is because no one is getting what they bargained for — they're getting *less* than they bargained for.

Dating today has become just another bait and switch technique. What you see is what you get, but what you get is not what you saw. Many people today are poor conductors in this regard. This is because people don't know who they are anymore, and if they do, shame keeps it in the closet. Left there too long and it will become Godzilla — some of you woke up one day and met him.

One of the main reasons for this is because no one defined them when they were young. If those who love us most do not correctly define us, we will forever roam the earth in search of the definition. In the search for our significance, our conduct becomes corroded because the inner value and beliefs remain for the most part, *undefined.* We then try to find our significance

10 The absolute latest annual divorce rate is 0.37% for the "year" ending Nov. 30, 2004. Since every divorce involves two people, the percentage becomes somewhat more meaningful if you double it. E.g., 0.74% of the entire population of married people gets divorced every year.

outside of ourselves as opposed to *inside* where it belongs. Those who know who they are (Because someone defined them) and embrace it, will have far more success than those who don't.

It's a problem when people look for their significance in substances, finances or some other inanimate object. Significance is *only* found in the heart of the God who created you. If you cannot see yourself as God sees you, you run the risk of becoming a vagabond and a wanderer like Cain[11] in the Genesis narrative or like Esau[12] who searched with tears for his father's blessing and no blessing was ever found — ever.

The Conviction Base

Conviction, simply put, is *why* we do it. Webster defines conviction as the *act* or process of convincing. Wow, that is amazing! The question is this: what are we trying to convince people of? I hate to keep saying this, but we are convincing others of what we believe through the intended or unintended act we do. Case in point, someone who wants to effectively convince another of what they believe about "horse training" may speak up when they see someone hitting a horse or using a negative form of training to gain the upper hand in a situation. You would say about that person that they were *convicted* when they saw the alleged abuse and therefore attempted to remedy the situation by aligning the circumstances to fit within their personal belief system.

People of preference will do nothing. Convictions are somewhat at odds with preferences; being that preferences are *second* and *third* choices that we tend to act upon based on the gravity of any given situation.

We must understand that preferences have not yet entered the realm of belief and become a foundational value, which is why they still remain within the area of choice. Back to the animal abuse example, depending on how stubborn a horse might become, you may have multiple levels of disciplinary actions at your disposal because you have not yet officially created a value on types of discipline for horses.

---

11 Cain is the first son of Adam and Eve, according to the Bible. He murdered his brother Able because of a combination of jealousy and being offended by God.
12 Genesis 25:19-25 narrates Esau's birth. He emerges from the womb with Jacob grasping his heel.

I know a gentleman who thought nothing of placing his Dalmatian in a headlock and pouring Tabasco Sauce down its throat for digging holes in the yard. He certainly had a conviction about not having holes dug in his yard. Needless to say, the dog never did it again. I on the other hand have some convictions concerning how far we should go when training an animal, which is why I spoke up about the matter when it happened.

Convictions are one's *only* choice, being that the value (On how we should treat animals) has been already *established*. This begs a question on many levels of the choice paradigm. For instance, pro-life people tend to act out of an *established* conviction. Saving the unborn life is the *only* choice available. The *choice* establishment will more or less trump the idea of having the option thus not establishing a conviction either way. The pro-choice model therefore does not fall under having a literal conviction because they don't call themselves pro-death meaning; destruction of the fetus is the *only* option.

One may argue that the pro-choice mind set has a conviction concerning one's ability to choose. This may be true, but they violate the Law of The Excluded Middle, which is one of the three fundamental laws of logic. They refuse to become hot or cold and so will ride the fence of neutrality for fear of being labeled as a minority on the matter by avoiding the real argument. Unfortunately, many on both sides of the issue use slight-of-word in order to mask a far more sinister agenda.

The pro-life people represent the child while the pro-choice people ignore the child and represent the mother. This is very interesting how one camp moves the argument from life and death to the ability to make choices for yourself; two separate ideas altogether. The argument should be about life and death in order to solve the abortion issue correctly and logically. Funny how nobody sees the fact that while the argument about how important it is to have the freedom to choose rages, the dear innocent child under discussion is completely left without the ability choose altogether. The real agenda for some (On both sides) is easy to uncover when the actions are observed across all the social issues involved.

A good example is one who claims to promote the protection of life, yet will blow up an abortion clinic to make their point, thus ending life in the process; this person is a lunatic. This violates the Square of Opposition in the world of logic and thus is no conviction at all. Others on the opposite side of the issue will promote choice when it comes to ending the lives of unborn children (Proving that they believe that the more developmentally able you are, the more important you become — scary), but will not regard the notion of choice when it comes to other issues such as the school voucher program where choice is a viable option.

Only those who are not paying attention will fall for this slight-of-word technique used on both sides of this issue. Adolph Hitler for example, represented a pro-death approach to unwanted races because it was a conviction within him — there was no other choice in the matter. He believed in what logic calls a universal negative when it came to the Jewish race and others. Those who fall into *Accidental Increase* tend to have a conviction no matter where they stand on the issue, be it for good or for bad.

The idea that someone is able to land the plane and settle the matter shows not only conviction, but also a resolute process of decision-making. People with strong resolve tend to do more by accident than those who still have not been able to come to a decision on particular matters regardless of the popularity or morality of the issue. Hitler, because of his extreme convictions, went from being a penniless vagrant eating in soup kitchens to nearly conquering the entire world, and all this with a very bad idea. He had more resolve for evil intent than most others had for good and therefore almost destroyed the entire world.

WWII thus became a battle of convictions between good and evil and you know the outcome. Thank God for the men and women who forcefully opposed his views with the sacrifice of their lives to prove it — *an act of conviction I might add.*

Being resolute is difficult for many because they fear offending others of a differing stance. These are those who live in the realm of preference. The homosexual movement in this country is a great example of another trend setting group gaining tremendous ground for the simple reason that *they are resolute.* People who only stand up when convenient[13] are a dime a dozen and so those who tend towards conviction must live inconvenient lives. The rarity is finding those who live with strong convictions and who also live *suc-*

---

13 Convenience & Conviction are polar opposites.

cessfully beside those with opposite beliefs. The key is keeping your convictions to yourself — *some of us need to retire from the job of being manager of the universe.*

You should be in control of your own life, not everyone else's life. This doesn't mean you don't take opportunity to share your ideas, it means you don't force them on everyone else like an idiot. Even the Christ allowed people to make their own decisions and he didn't apologize for it. It takes EQ (Emotional Quotient), IQ (Information Quotient) and CQ[14] (Character Quotient) to balance your social interactions properly.

One of my favorite personas is *American Idol's* Simon Cowell.[15] Why are we all drawn to him in particular? Besides being a rebel, Simon is completely resolute in his decision-making ability. This year we all watched as he lowered the hammer when deciding a potential Idol's fate during the new "saving" process that the producers instituted. If you're a fan of the show (as I am) you'll notice that Paula's[16] *emotions* always end up dictating her responses, thus circumventing that which she internally finds resolute, but externally is unable to bring to bear. This may be why Simon will gross over forty million while Paula will make less than five for doing the same show.

Sure, there may be other reasons for the pay differentiation, but I firmly believe that the bottom line is because Simon is completely resolute in his decision-making ability. This same ability affects his entire life and work no matter what it is. The fact is this — he is where he is because of at least *some* of these truths. If you follow his story, you will see that he is successful by accident. In his early life, he took menial jobs but never got along with coworkers or his bosses (That's a big surprise!). This makes sense if you've ever seen him on the show. His father secured him a position at EMI Music Publishing[17] working in the *mail room*[18] of all places. Simon attended Dover College but dropped out early. It doesn't seem to matter though, does it? If you are going to take anything away from this section, let it be this; land your plane.

---

14 Another one of my fascinatingly true bright ideas.
15 **Simon Phillip Cowell** (born October 7, 1959) is an English television personality, A&R executive, television producer, idiot and entrepreneur.
16 **Paula Julie Abdul** (born June 19, 1962) is an American pop singer, record producer, dancer, choreographer, actress, airhead and television personality.
17 **The EMI Group** (Electric & Musical Industries Ltd.) is a British music company.
18 This is where a lot of accidents that end up creating increase happen.

Accidental Increase takes place when we are bold and resolute about where we stand in life. Be either black or white; don't mute your shade so as to leave everyone wondering (Including you!). This isn't about being a jerk; it's about being clear. Life is like a hockey game — the thicker the ice, the more you can pay attention to what you are doing. This combined with knowing your position will create an advantage. If you don't know where you stand on the issues of life, it's like playing hockey on thin ice as well as not knowing your position on the team. You end up so preoccupied with the idea of potentially falling through the ice and making a wrong move that you can't concentrate on making a goal.

I remember playing town sports as a kid and not knowing what I was supposed to do; it was a terrible sinking feeling when things started to move in my direction. Marry that girl and stop wasting her time! Start fielding resumes so you can trust God and quit that job that you hate so much! Try out for that position, move to Indiana — whatever it is that you consistently won't do, but constantly think about; do it for heaven's sake. Stop blaming everyone else for your lack of resolve and make a conscious decision to move forward with your gut feelings. You don't want to be lying upon your death-bed counting your could a-should a-would a's.

We've only got one go of it folks; make it count. Some of you need to go back to school and finish your degree while others need to take some time off and go on that humanitarian adventure you're always thinking about. Some of you need to go to Walmart and buy some spine. Remember, the fence is a painful place to sit; the sooner you pick a side of the fence and jump, the better you'll feel.

2

The Achievement Gap

The Power of Receiving

"Most people are bothered by those passages of Scripture they do not understand, but the passages that bother me are those I do understand."
—MARK TWAIN

One of the greatest mysteries of all time is what I have come to call the achievement gap.[1] I first noticed this principle while preparing for a message I was to speak in the late 80's. One of the examples I was going to use in my talk was found in the Old Testament of the Christian Bible and surrounded the life of David, the boy who was to become king. Here is what I found…

The David and Saul Principle

After reading about David[2] and his weird relationship with King Saul in the Bible, I came away with a very interesting piece of information. *Saul*

---

1 I came up with this bright idea in 1989 and it has altered my life.
2 David was the second king of the United Kingdom of Israel according to the Hebrew Bible/Old Testament.

"In today's culture we tend to reward talent, not faithfulness. We tend to look for *a*-bility instead of *sta*-bility."

was an achiever, but David was a receiver. It was a quite fascinating concept, but it was as true as me writing this right now. *David did more by accident than Saul did by purpose.* Many academics will speak of David as a cunning warrior or some genius battle planner, but to be honest, David worked at Burger King®.[3] Don't get me wrong, he was definately tough, but more importantly, David was a shepherd, not a military genius. David had conviction, which ran through his veins like a freight train. David was known for minding his business, not jockeying for position. When King Saul was depressed, he asked one of his servants if he knew of anyone who could play an instrument because he thought it would cheer him up. His servant told him about David, "*Who is with the sheep*," not sharpening his axe or showcasing his military prowess.

David was a sheepherder and he was *faithful*. Looking at the story, you can see David always doing what his father asked of him *without* complaint. In today's culture we tend to reward talent, not faithfulness. We tend to look for *a*-bility instead of *sta*-bility. I don't know about you, but I've always found it much easier to make a faithful person able, as opposed to making an able person faithful.

When Saul and the Israelites were encamped in the Valley of Elah and had drawn up a battle line in order to meet their archenemy the Philistines, David was acting as water boy for those on the front line — mainly his brothers, who were preparing for the ensuing battle. David's father Jesse asked him to take some bread and cheese to the commander of the unit and also to check on his brothers. As usual, David followed orders. Early the next morning, David loaded up and set out as his father had directed. Ironically enough, he arrived at the camp just as the men were taking up their battle positions and shouting the war cry.

Here's where it starts to get real interesting. David runs to greet his brothers and begins a short conversation with them when Goliath,[4] the super-sized Philistine champion, starts shouting his usual defiant mockery

---

3 My first real job was at Burger King.
4 Some historians claim Goliath (a nephilim leftover) was nearly 13 feet tall.

against the men of Israel and their God. This is where one can find the best four-word statement ever allowed to slip from the writer's pen: *"...and David heard it."* I just love that line.

I dare to say that David not only heard it, he *felt* it. The Philistine champion's retorts violated David's conscience to the core. Those words must have cut across his heart like an axe to his femur. At that moment, David asked, *"What will be done for the man who removes this disgrace from Israel?"* I wish I were there to witness this conscience driven freak boy who would not standby and allow the Philistine champion to defy the armies of his God.

While every soldier ran in the other direction, David stood firm. David was discussing the short future of the disgraceful Goliath of Gath,[5] when his oldest brother Eliab heard him speaking and *"burned with anger"* against David. This is sibling rivalry at its best (or worst). Eliab lays into David, calling him conceited, wicked and reckless. Typical!

I had always found this piece of the story puzzling until I figured out what was really going on. David reacts immediately by asking, "now what have I done?" This phrase lets us in on the fact that this must have been commonplace. The unfaithful always find fault with the faithful.

His oldest brother knew that David was such a better man than he, even though he was still young. David had more courage and determination than anyone he knew, and was about to show them all his quality. David wasn't trying to be brave. He was brave at heart (Possibly the original Brave Heart?)!

"Courage is not the absence of fear, it is the absence of self,"[6] and this was something his brothers knew nothing about. David was just being true to whom he was and in that process, it accidentally thrust him onto the world stage. David's life from this point forward unfolds through a series of similar events, which eventually creates a synergistic momentum that brings uncommon valor and remarkable increase. He eventually became the greatest king that Israel ever had. Imagine that, from Burger King® to Mighty King!

---

5 I'd rather run a shovel through my pelvis than have to live in a place called "Gath."
6 Another unbelievable quote from *Irwin Raphael McManus* of Mosaic Church, California. Mosaic.org.

"The most successful people I know achieved their success, not by the "Lone Ranger" approach, but by the "Lone Ranger and Tonto" approach."

Receiving Your Way to the Top

Understanding the difference between achieving and receiving is a must for success. There are two kinds of people in this world, the *givers* and the *takers*. I want to ask you this straight up. You ready? Are you a giver or are you a taker? This is an important question and deserves full attention. The principle of achievement is built upon "self-energy" and "self-interest." These are not bad qualities. They just are not fundamentally powerful.

Our society is constantly becoming more and more convoluted as we continue to move forwards in the post-modern era. A gentleman I know once said, "*The bird that flies in ever tightening circles eventually flies up its own orifice and disappears.*"[7]

When focusing on achieving, we must understand that all achievement is selfish. According to Webster's Dictionary, the word "*selfish*" is defined as: "*concerned chiefly or only with oneself.*" This does not mean that we are never to try to achieve goals or success, but we must first define how we are going to move from point A to point B. This "movement" is the achieving process. Successful people are always including others in their achievement.

The most successful people I know achieved their success, not by the "Lone Ranger" approach, but by the "Lone Ranger and Tonto" approach. Doing this enables them to reap the benefits of others' abilities and gifting along with their own. The successful attack problems and challenges not independently of others, but *through* others. When you bring others into the mix, you not only strengthen your possibilities of achievement, but also become a *contributor* rather than simply a *controller*. The principles of giving and sharing are timeless and are indifferent to our own opinions about them. If we tap into the power of sharing responsibility or achieving success through others, we then embark on a journey potentially worth millions — and I don't mean just money.

---

7 *Bob Mumford* is a dynamic Bible teacher with a unique and powerful gift that defies reason. Be careful, he might be an idiot sometimes as I am at times.

When we work together, all individuals become receptors and are challenged to cooperate and exchange ideas (or gifts) with one another. In very much the same way, when we choose not to participate in this scenario, we *take* from those around us to help facilitate our own desires. This proves to be lonely and unproductive to say the least. David accomplished everything through people. He couldn't keep them away if he tried. When King Saul's jealousy reached its pinnacle, he went after David with a vengeance and ultimately made 21 attempts to kill him. David, like cream, kept rising to the top no matter what Saul did and even proved his *Accidental Increase* in his series of escapes from Saul's menacing grasp.

His loyalty attracted loyal friends, as Saul's *own son* Jonathan found his way into David's heart when he heard David speaking with his father on one occasion. Jonathan and David thus end up cutting an ancient Hebrew Covenant with each other - the closest of all ancient pacts. We see that Jonathan became a quick ally to David and told him he would do anything in his power to help him. David's fame spread all the way to Gath and reached Achish. In fact, the king of Gath heard the rumors of how much better a warrior David was than Saul — this story just keeps getting more and more crazy. This frightened David and so he pretended to be insane in front of the king of Gath and his men in an attempt to save his own life.

You might note how David shied away from fame, whereas Saul reveled in it. When David left Gath after his insanity plea, he escaped to a cave in Adullam. It wasn't long before his father Jesse and others heard about this and assembled about four hundred men who were discontented, distressed and in debt (Great group of folks here). This rabble wasn't exactly the "who's who" in Jerusalem! They all joined him there begging him to lead them. David couldn't lose for winning. Here is a man running from leadership, but unable to get away from it because it is pursuing him so relentlessly. Upon reading this, I came to the conclusion that we should never give titles to those who want them. I always keep my eyes open for those who take responsibility without all the fanfare and flattering titles. Those people are your best choices for leadership. David never went after the Kingship; the Kingship went after David.

A Man's Gift Makes Room for Him

David's son, the wise King Solomon spoke in one of his ancient proverbs about a man's gift making room for him.[8] This is the art of receiving. Many will try to make room for their gift, but it will never work. Your gifts make room for you and if they don't then you are either not ready or you just flat don't have the gifts you had hoped — so what! Greatness is received, not achieved. If you have achieved it, then you have simply succeeded at making yourself important and everyone fell for it. The first time I ever spoke publicly, was to a crowd of 300 or more. I was so scared that I started crying right there on the spot! I was but 23 years old then. I am now 45 and get just as scared (Minus the crying) whenever I am asked to speak.

"Greatness is received, not achieved. If you have achieved it, then you have simply succeeded at making yourself important and everyone fell for it."

Don't chase your dreams like Saul chased his; let your dreams chase you. The problem I see these days is that more and more people are insecure and therefore operating out of a *need* mentality. If I want a wife, I'll find a good one. If I *need* a wife, I'll settle for the first one who comes along. Need-based thinkers *always* make poor decisions. Someone who needs a drug fix will steal from their own grandma! Never marry because you *need* a husband or wife, marry because you *want* one. Needs are insatiable — a black hole; no thing and no person will be able to fill it; that's God's job.

Faithful in need

Notice how in the David story that he was faithful to all those who joined him in Adullam's cave even though he himself was running for his own life. Again, David was faithful in need. Faithful to others' needs while he was in desperate need himself. This is the making of a true king. Those who accidentally increase always place the needs of others ahead of their own. They

---

8 Proverbs 18:16

may complain and get angry with others, but when the chips are down they set aside personal ambition for the sake of those who really need. These are those who enter relationships for what they can bring to the table, not for what they receive at the table.

I'll never forget the time when I was about six months out of seminary and taking on the role as senior pastor for a small group of people totaling about 18 members. This grew rapidly to about 50 or 60 members within a four-month period. It had started out as a coffee house ministry focusing on music, stories and having a place for unfortunate folks to express themselves and feel accepted. Later, the president of the ministry thought about making it into something a bit more. The regular attendees were interested in forming a formal church out of the small group and wanted someone they could count on for counseling and regular teaching. The goal was to bring in someone to pastor the people and ultimately branch off and become an autonomous 501C3 entity once the group was well established.

That's when I was phoned. Hunted down, actually. I was living in Tulsa at the time when my wife and I were invited to fly to Massachusetts to speak to that small group about four months prior to my scheduled graduation. Upon arrival, I assessed the group for its emotional heartbeat and determined it to be a perfect setting for a minister just starting out. This was an excellent opportunity for me to invest into the lives of some wonderful, albeit wounded people. This was an answer to months of praying in secret for an opportunity to share the message of wholeness to a broken generation of people upon my graduation. It was a freezing cold Valentine's Day in 1987 I was 24 years old. I was subsequently hired that weekend and would return the following June for proper installation upon completing my studies.[9]

After settling into a small musty basement apartment where we actually had mushrooms growing on the walls, approximately six months into my work I had to deal with a problem I saw emerging within the small group dynamic. It involved the leader who invited me to pastor and another female person. This issue was becoming a growing concern and I felt that if it were not addressed, the fallout would be devastating. After making the decision to go ahead and deal with it as best I knew how, I went out with the leader and

---

9 I graduated with about a 3.6 GPA, yea! That's up from a good solid "C."

decided I would just tell him head-on what I thought and why (either/or). That particular decision would later become the pivotal point between utter ruin and everything I had endeavored to accomplish. The leader's menacing strategy after that meeting was to begin a series of visits to each member of the small group detailing my so-called ambitions to form a cult that would eventually be the undoing of everyone involved.

After seasoning (poisoning) the members with just enough misinformation to cause them to raise questions, one faithful person called me on the phone and told me of the devious plot. At that juncture, I called the leader and outright asked him if this was true. He responded by saying, "we need to meet in person and discuss your future with this ministry." We met at a local restaurant and he looked me in the eyes and told me, "If you want to remain a part of this ministry, then I suggest you do things my way around here."[1] Yikes!

It was at this moment that I realized he was challenging me to compromise everything I have always believed in. I was being forced to make a choice — an only choice. Not being able to change my value base, the core emotional driving structure of my being and purpose, the amount of options I had at my disposal was instantly reduced to one — NO! I had to resign my first pastorate in what looked like a scandalous failure in leadership.

I decided to call my closest friend in Ohio whom I met at school several years earlier. My friend listened in silence as I began to articulate my verbal assault on the leader and his devious scheme. I explained to him all the sordid details and in the process unloaded with all eagerness my disgust with the leadership and the situation as a whole. This is when my faithful friend decided that it was time to let me in on my own beliefs.

"Remember the discussion we had several months back when you talked about walking in love towards those who despitefully use you and betray you? You should listen to your own teachings." Ouch!

He then began instructing me about my behavior and how calling him up and assaulting this man's character over the phone was not in line with what I claimed I believed. I lowered my head and in a whimpering voice replied, "You're right." After that night, I assembled a group of men and re-

---

1 The words of a fool. One who is self interested and extremely self absorbed; God have mercy on his eternal soul for abusing innocent followers and children-yikes!

turned to the building and we painted the entire inside as a favor. A few months later I was able to leave that town in peace. It wasn't until 15 years later however that I actually emotionally faced that situation head-on and forgave that leader from my heart. Better late than never I suppose.

I had carried that wound around with me long enough. I am forever grateful for that faithful friend who, at the possible expense of our relationship, told me the hard truth. He truly sacrificed his "self" by being willing to look like a jerk. He put the facts before his feelings in an attempt to save me from my own hypocrisy.[2] Was I justified in being angry? Absolutely! Was I justified in behaving in a manner that was inconsistent with what I believed (my labeling) and so eloquently instructed others to believe? Absolutely not! If I am unable to view myself in the mirror of reality and come away with the truth about what I see, then I should not be in a position of asking others to do the same. Don't get me wrong, this was a very difficult thing to do and on top of that, I didn't want to do it. But I just couldn't get away from the idea of being honest with myself. I was in need of comfort, but what I needed more was character. I received a gift of money in the mail the following week from someone 1300 miles away who didn't even know the situation! We used that to start our own ministry with the three folks who remained and ended up pastoring for another few years before leaving the state.

After working 50 hours a week painting and spending the rest of my time with a small parish, I completely burned myself out at the ripe old age of 27. Little did I know that those days were exactly what I needed and would prove to be one of the best bad accidents I ever had.

People claiming to be ministers should not act the way these terrible people acted; nor should the local policeman be snorting coke, but these things will always be prevalent where people are involved. Another key to *Accidental Increase* is your ability to never hold the profession hostage because of the monkeys[3] who make their way into it. You will always have crooked cops, pastors, priests, doctors and lawyers, but this is never a reason not to visit the hospital, courtroom or church.

The ability to separate these issues from individual persons will lend you a leg up in this world. If you are one who refuses to attend church be-

---

2 It appears that if I don't check in with myself regularly, I become a hypocrite by default.
3 People who overdose on "Stupid Pills" and then mysteriously end up in a profession.

cause of the apparent and obvious hypocrisy of some, then consider the words of the Christ who called these people hypocrites, snakes and white-washed tombs who's walls have been painted with a fine white finish, but who's interiors housed the dead.[4] Even he himself did not condone the hypocritical spirits of unjust freaks among us, and so to claim refusal to play for the hypocritical team defies logic seeing that through this behavior you end up actually captain of the team you hate.

The Self-Subtraction Principle

If you spend all your time trying to do great, you will be hard pressed to be great. This is the difference between a human being and a human doing. Human beings just are. They are not over achievers. They have a sense of contentment about them. If you are consistently discontented and always trying to self promote, you've got issues. Solomon said to "let another praise you, and not your own mouth; someone else, and not your own lips."[5] He also said, "The crucible for silver and the furnace for gold, *but man is tested by the praise he receives*."[6] What we don't sometimes realize is that we are praising ourselves. Praise can be poison if you are not careful.

Some people have a very strong need orientation and thus end up sucking the life out of everyone else around them for need of constant affirmation. People see them coming and they run for the hills!

Those who increase are always a breath of fresh air. They bring life with them wherever they go. They consistently bring value by seeing the value in others without realizing their own value. *This is the self-subtraction principle.* The power of self-subtraction eliminates the power of others in regards to emotionally holding you hostage to your own faults. Let me explain; I call this *adversarial agreement.* Jesus, during one of his first century teachings, said, "*agree with your enemy while you are on the way...*"[7] This statement literally means to throw the fight, admit defeat — take the dive. Lay down.

4 Matthew 23:27
5 Proverbs 27:2
6 Proverbs 27:21
7 Matthew 5:25

Our nature is to make the other fall down and not lay down ourselves or to blame the other person or party. Jesus chose to lay down his life so that others would not fall down. Christ's principle is this; *every death is followed by a resurrection*. I heard an interesting story many years ago about the mountain goat. If two mountain goats are coming towards each other and cannot pass one another without one careening down the cliff, an amazing thing will happen. One of the goats will lay prostrate and the other will walk over it in order to save them both. We will never rise up if we are not capable of first falling down. *Intentional dives make for an unintentional rise.*[8] Never forget that! Preserve the dignity and measure of others, not self. If you seek to rescue and deliver others as surely as you live, you yourself will be rescued. Refusing this mode of operation will imprison you just as Jesus said it would.

Allow yourself to be an instrument for the preservation of others, not for *self*-preservation — that's stupid. The famed speaker and author Zig Ziglar[9] made this point clear years ago; "*...help others get what they want and you will always get what you need.*" You become successful by helping others become successful. You will know you have accidentally succeeded when you find yourself saying; "*How did I get here?*" Selfish ambition is no match when it comes to humble increase.

When we constantly live a life of self-focus and convoluted intention, we negate the power and freedom available to us through selflessness. Christ is our model for such behavior. His focus was always outward. He was the opposite of an emotionally disadvantaged person. He was a life giving spirit. If we are to succeed socially, we must first jump the hurdle of addition and embrace subtraction; we must allow ourselves to be expensed during the process of human interaction. One of the greatest statements ever penned was written in a first century epistle called the letter to the Galatians. In this letter, the author claims, "*I no longer live...*"[10] This is the ultimate self subtractive position. The ability to get along without constant emotional stimulation brings health and well being not only to you, but also to those around you.

---

8 This truth is self evident. It will happen sooner or later if one continues this as a way of life — believe me, I know.
9 "Zig" Ziglar (6 November 1926) is an American author, salesperson, and motivational speaker. His latest book (as of 2007) is; *God's Way Is Still the Best Way*.
10 Galatians 2:20

Self-centeredness keeps us from seeing and experiencing the world around us as well as appreciating its beauty and abundance.

The constant focus on self makes for self-destructiveness on many levels. This singular attentiveness disables our ability to engage with others in a positive manner, which is where true happiness really lies. We find ourselves focused entirely on personal trivial points of interest and therefore miss all the cues necessary for relationship management and social accountability and interaction. Self-subtraction is all about taking *you* out of the equation. It's about selfless living and responding to the social needs around us without personal protectionism. Now here's what I want you to come away with. We are all guilty of visiting the achievement camp, but some of us live there. I have been telling people for years, *"It's not wrong to be wrong, it's wrong to stay wrong."*[11] So it is also with the achievement gap. It's okay to visit, but it's not a good idea to live there. None of us are perfect. Stop chasing your future and you'll run right into it in time — your destiny is looking for you. Let it find you minding your own business.

Hostages Takers

After reading the last few pages, you may have landed your plane on the same field that I am on regarding achieving and receiving dynamics. The interesting thing about the aforementioned King David is that although he was in significant need, i.e. running for his life from Saul, he still remained faithful to those in greater need. This is what I call being faithful in need. I say this again because I believe it bears repeating. Those who are faithful in need remain attached to the needs of others while in greater need themselves in at least a few areas. Accidental increase takes place when you are mindful of others while being needful yourself. This doesn't mean we neglect personal responsibility, but rather act responsibly in accordance to others while maintaining our own affairs.

It's difficult to go through life maintaining our own affairs let alone the affairs of others. But, when we are able to balance the notion surrounding the sustenance of others with our own, we become far more effective

---

11 I heard this statement slip from the lips of one of my all time best friends Adam Boyd in 1992.

in this life. I have found this out through maintaining a life of being aware of those around me. My wife has placed a saying in our kitchen that reads; "*Live simply that others may simply live,*" and I believe this actually sums up my thoughts on this matter fairly well. You may be wondering if there are times when I don't want to share my hard earned resources with others and to that I say *all the time*. I find that I have to make a conscious decision to do the right thing each and every time something like this comes up. You must remember this one thing; it's the *right* thing, not *every* thing. Keeping things in perspective will help you become successful in this area.

A very dear friend once gave me some great advice; he told me to never forget to count the o's. Ask yourself this; "Is it good or is it God?"[12] Too many o's can create a very big problem in the long run no matter how wonderful what you are doing appears to be. Even the Christ didn't deal with everyone, but he was always dealing with someone.

What I am not advocating here is a welfare mentality that enables others to shirk their own personal responsibilities. I remember having a heated discussion with an individual concerning another person whom I felt was acting irresponsibly in a certain situation. It wasn't long thereafter that I found out the "suspect" individual was facing a delinquent mortgage payment. The next time I saw him I asked him how he was doing and he reluctantly informed me of his depressing situation. Funny thing is, after a 15-minute engagement, I found myself writing him a check for the difference on his mortgage payment. I realize now that although I had difficulty with some particulars surrounding his poor decision making skills, I wasn't going to become a dog to prove it. This is the difference my friend; being able to separate between past poor decision-making and present needs that are out of someone's control. Although this person didn't seem to be the brightest bulb on the tree concerning past performance, it was unjust to rate him that way for his present situation. It appears that many of us like to hold people hostage to past poor decisions in an attempt to make them pay for their previous acts of stupidity.

The higher road is to be able to distinguish between the *outright* stupid decisions and the *seemingly* stupid decisions that people are forced to make

12 Thank you Johnny Snellgrove.

because of outside influences more or less out of their control. This may at times make you feel as though helping is rewarding poor performance, but only self-interested people think this way. If your act of kindness becomes a showcase for your so-called benevolent lifestyle then your motives are backwards. Every situation and every person deserves a clean slate before investigation. This proves that you have the ability to walk in a state of forgiveness as opposed to being one who holds grudges and set's himself up as the "Motives Police." People who hold grudges do not increase very well. I have found that people deserve second and third chances - myself included!

If there's one thing I can't stand, it's false advertisement. Many people will showcase their giving and helping of others in an attempt to promote themselves in life. This is sad. Their benevolence is nothing more than a personal self-help program funded by their own pocket book. We help others because it's right — period.

I'll never forget when I was mowing a neighbor's lawn each Saturday because he was just flat too old to do it himself. An individual from my church told me one day that he heard of my act of kindness and said; "That's an awesome plan Steve!" Sadly, he assumed I was just trying to "get him to church" — yuck! His reverting to life's lowest level of knowledge (Assumption) disallowed him to understand exactly who I am. The fact is, he just needed his grass cut. I wasn't on a mission to "convert" his poor soul; that's not my job. My job is to treat him with dignity and respect, like I would want to be treated — no strings attached. We must be content with just doing what is right without the fanfare. Those who can do this tend to increase more rapidly in areas of joy *and* contentment. Somebody once said that Godliness combined with contentment is a great gain.[13] And you know what? I agree.

---

13 St. Paul writing young Timothy who was about 17 years old in 1 Timothy 6:6

3

Ethocentrism

The Power of Ethos

"Eros will have naked bodies; Friendship naked personalities."
—C. S. Lewis

The Power of Ethos

Aristotle, in his Rhetoric, which was published more than three centuries before Christ, noted the effectiveness of individuals involved in the persuasive process (those speaking with the intent to persuade another). Thus he developed a comprehensive theory on rhetorical thought.[1] This theory has been the fundamental stratagem for communication ever since. What Aristotle reasoned was that communication takes place between three separate entities — the one speaking, the one listening and the message itself or the ethos, pathos and logos.

He theorized that the process of persuasion was an interaction between these three parts. All three need to be present and all three need to

---

1 Aristotle's Rhetoric is an ancient Greek treatise on the art of persuasion, dating from the fourth century BCE.

be authentic. The ethos piece I will contemplate is the most important of all three. Ethos can be described as the character or disposition of a community, group or person or the fundamental values peculiar to any specific person or group. Ethos is about the underlying sentiment that forms the belief system of any person.

What Aristotle believed was if the person or group you were endeavoring to persuade believed you to be authentic, informed, knowledgeable, virtuous, trustworthy and concerned about the welfare of the recipient, then you were probably right. A fascinating example of this is found in CS Lewis' *Chronicles of Narnia*. In it, the youngest character Lucy travels to an unlikely world called Narnia and later recounts her journey to her unbelieving sister and brothers. Over time, despite her implausible tale, she is proven to be credible while her older brother Edmund proves that he lacks credibility altogether.

Are you credible? Credibility is an intrinsic value that many people today lack. Helmut Thielicke,[2] a famous German theologian, believed credibility to be the main operational piece within a communicator's ethos. He theorized that the process of persuasion was an interaction between these three parts. All three need to be present and all three need to be authentic.

Credibility can be defined as the capability of being believed or what makes one worthy of belief or confidence. Those who are credible contain the quality or power to elicit belief from others who may not have even considered believing what you propose. This is an amazing element. George G. Hunter III, Distinguished Professor of Church Growth and Evangelism at Asbury Theological Seminary, writes about the ethos of St. Patrick in his remarkable book entitled; *The Celtic Way of Evangelism*. He attributes St. Patrick's high ethos as to the reason for his unrivaled effect on the Irish.

Just like St. Patrick, Accidental Increase takes place when those whom you interact with from day to day consider you credible. Here's where it gets a little weird though. Many believe they have to be *incredible* in order to pull this off! Flatly, this is not true.

Credible carries far more worth than the *incredible* carries. This is true in all facets of life. Those who endeavor to share their Christian faith will

---

2 Helmut Thielicke (December 4, 1908 in Wuppertal — March 5, 1986 in Hamburg) was a German theologian and rector of the University of Hamburg from 1960 to 1978.

many times try to represent the Christ in incredible ways rather than just simply being credible with those whom they love and care for. Perhaps this is the problem — the loving and caring column is a little short. If it becomes far more important for you to display incredible feats rather than simply being a credible witness, then your issues are running deeper than you may be willing to state.

> "If it becomes far more important for you to display incredible feats rather than simply being a credible witness, then your issues are running deeper than you may be willing to state."

I have never had to struggle with being a representation of the God that I serve. This is primarily because I do not set out to prove his existence to those whom I connect with. Come to think of it, I never really think about it. This is probably why I find success in relationships without my faith becoming a nuisance in the process. If you are caring in order to make points with God or people, you will find difficulty in relationship maneuvering. Your caring for others must eliminate yourself from the equation, not create additional perks for you in the process.

Most people can readily pick out those who are in relationship with them for selfish reasons. They will end up rejecting the relationship based on the person's lack of ethos. The power of ethos will actually reach a destination before you do. When people talk about an individual's reputation preceding them, they are actually speaking about their ethos going before them and paving the way for goodness or ill will. When Hunter speaks of St. Patrick in his book entitled; *The Celtic Way of Evangelism*, he makes reference to his ethos reaching the villages before he did. Patrick really did love the Irish and his success was an automatic result of his tremendous ethos.

The famed Scottish missionary David Livingstone[3] sailed for Africa in the year 1840 after much preparation by the London Missionary Society. He spent the first 12 years caring for the natives. He taught the Gospel and trained them in the habits of honesty and industry. Few men since the days

3 David Livingstone (19 March 1813—1 May 1873) was a Scottish Congregationalist pioneer medical missionary with the London Missionary Society and explorer in Central Africa.

of the apostles have done more for this hurting world than did David Livingstone. Honors came to him, but he did not allow them to turn or distract him from the mission of duty. To the end, he kept the simple faith and the humble heart of a dear child. On the morning of May 1, 1873, an African boy found him dead on his knees in a position of prayer for the African people. The natives were so broken by his death that they prepared his body so *"that the white chief may be buried among his own people."* They also removed his heart that it might be buried in the land and among the people that he loved. His spirit is well represented in the words from his last letter, which are inscribed upon his tomb:

"May heaven's richest blessing come down on every one, English, American or Turk, who will help to heal the open sore of the world."

David Livingstone's' ethos lives to this day. It echoes from his heart still buried among the people he loved. Interestingly enough, by the year 2020 Africa may be the most Christian continent on the face of the earth.

The Power of Knowledge

Some say knowledge is power, but I say knowledge can be powerful depending on the motive for sharing it. Though knowing things is important, being known far outweighs it. Take the late Mother Theresa for instance. She was far more *known* than she was known for *knowing*. Even Solomon says, *"A wise man has great power, and a man of knowledge increases strength."*[4] What we need to understand is that although knowledge is important, it isn't *all*-important. Even the Apostle Paul claimed that although knowledge puffs a person up (This is the person with the information), it was *love* that built the receiver up. Anybody who knows anything knows it's not what you know, but whom you know. After all, how do you get to heaven? There are two kinds of knowledge I want to discuss here — knowing *why* and knowing *how*.

The person who knows how has a job, but the person who knows why is the boss. Those who increase never spend inordinate amounts of time telling you how (think about people who are always telling you how to do things

---

4 Proverbs 24:5

better). How annoying! These people are however, informative. Those who spend more time on the why will have far more success over the long term because those who know why are truly wise. There is a stark difference between the wise and the informed. The how people are teachers, the why people are mentors. It's the difference between school and apprenticeship. While the teacher style is very *informative*, the mentor style is *interactive*. It's

> "The *how* people are teachers, the *why* people are mentors. It's the difference between school and apprenticeship."

the interaction with others that brings the better result when engaging with other people. At times the how engagement can come across as condescending while the why engagement is seen as supportive and personable.

I would suggest that those who increase tend to be mentors. Solomon says, "*Reckless words pierce like a sword, but the tongue of the wise brings healing.*"[5] Knowledge must be tempered with emotional intelligence. Experts claim that your IQ[6] is pretty much set in stone by the age of 14. Therefore the increase in smarts after that point is nothing more than being further informed. Most people can gather additional facts and figures as they grow older, but few seem to gain the ability to initiate, apply and integrate that information in a way that promotes the welfare of others.

Do you have the rare ability to share your knowledge without the recipient feeling uninformed or stupid? When you recover from the how mentality, you must uncover the hidden potential of mentoring and discover the hidden potential in others because It will create tremendous increase in the lives of others and in yours as well! This is a gift.

I can count on one hand the people who have a way of increasing your knowledge base while still magically creating a sense of importance within you in the process. Then there are those who hoard information and make you jump hoops in order to have some of it. They constantly remind you where you got it from.[7]

---

5 Proverbs 12:18
6 The term "IQ" from the German Intelligenz-Quotient, was coined by the German psychologist William Stern in 1912
7 Possibly a former graduate of "Moron School."

Many people view knowledge as a way of gaining the upper hand in conversation or having a superior position in the emotional arena of discussion. These people are insecure, but will use their brainpower to keep themselves emotionally elevated when engaging others. They may also deem certain people as *unworthy* of the coveted information and will therefore cherry pick those who they will allow special access.

This way of thinking goes back centuries and can be seen among the ancient Gnostics[8] who believed they held secret information and therefore kept it from the masses in an attempt to differentiate themselves. They would only consider initiates and selected individuals who they deemed worthy to access the special information. Those who live a life of Accidental Increase don't hoard information or hide it; they share it openly and willingly. It has been said that a wise man keeps his knowledge to himself. This is profound but not altogether accurate at first glance because knowledge is a tool useful for helping, not hurting. Those who keep their knowledge to themselves *and* are wise, are those who refuse to arrogantly gush information for selfish or prideful reasons.

The emotionally intelligent person knows when to pull information out, how to apply it and when to put it away while the recipient remains clueless as to what just happened. Knowledge is not something to capitalize on, but rather it is a useful tool in bringing about harmony to those who are expending their full attention. Instead of saying; "It's not what you know, but whom you know," I would say; "It's not what you know, but how you share what you know." To bring you back to our first point within this section "Is knowledge power?" No, but knowledge can be powerful. It all depends on who's wielding it.

The Power of Persuasion

In his book, Influence, *The Psychology of Persuasion*, Dr. Robert B. Cialdini[9] introduces the six weapons of influence used in persuasion. They

---

8 Greek: knowledge. A group of freaks that thought secret knowledge was better than a good wife, great food and a reasonably fun job.
9 Robert B. Cialdini is a social psychologist that is currently Regents' Professor of Psychology and W.P. Carey Distinguished Professor of Marketing at Arizona State University where he has also been named Distinguished Graduate Research Professor.

are *reciprocation, consistency, social proof, liking, authority* and *scarcity*. Some can wield these tools with great precision, but more importantly, some wield them by accident. These are the ones we will discuss here. Those who use these principles without a manipulative agenda tend to reap an amazing return on their inadvertent investment. When I discovered this book several years ago, I was amazed at how many of these principles were at work within my own life and was surprised to find that they had a name. A few of the examples used here were taken from Dr. Robert B. Cialdini's insights into these six rules.

The Reciprocity Rule

Let's begin with the reciprocation principle. Several years ago, a university professor demonstrated astonishing results from a remarkable experiment. He sent Christmas cards to a sample of perfect strangers. What followed was a surprising response. Total strangers returned the nicety with cards addressed to him personally — a man they neither had met nor knew. They did not know where he came from or who he was. What took place is what is known as the reciprocity rule, a formidable tool for getting results on purpose. What happens is the following: if an individual receives a valuable from anyone, they feel the automatic human need to reciprocate or give back. The beauty of this action is that many do this without realizing it and it becomes paramount in increasing their success. This has been something I have done for years without knowing I was actually doing it.

Just recently, I was spending a little time each month connecting with clients just because I like them. Through this process, one of my clients sent me an e-mail asking; *"Would you please bill us for all the extra work you are doing? We want to pay it."* So I drafted a bill for a reasonable amount and they paid it immediately along with a thank you note!

This was something I neither planned nor understood — I just thought to myself, "Wow! What great clients." What they were thinking was, "Wow! What a great consultant!" I just thought I was being friendly — they perceived me as bringing something far more valuable than just friendship, *I was meeting a need.* Those who succeed selling by accident are people who do not actually sell; they influence — I was influencing people. If a telemarketer[10] has ever harassed you then you know what I mean; they are not influencing me at all, they are usually angering me. Half the time, they don't even know my name! This is the worst representation a company can offer, but will never cease doing because it works *most* of the time.

High influencers "sell" accidentally. Low influencers turn you off. What I mean is everything is not a sales pitch when it comes to the high influence person who is operating out of *Accidental Increase*. They bring valuable information to the conversation without strategizing in an attempt to get you to buy. They make your life easier and more productive for free! When this happens, people inquire of it because it's so rare. Have you ever been to a car dealership and seen the human vultures (salespeople) in the windows waiting to pounce? Yuck! The fact is, every time I have purchased a vehicle, I always looked for a salesman when I had a question. I am just like you and everyone else. If you act like a kitten, people will come pet you but if you act like a vulture, they'll probably want to shoot you! Being valuable therefore, is one of the greatest influential bullets of all time.

You should be influencing people for the better not for the worse. If you are in the business of sales or affecting people with a service of some sort, your clients should be excited to see you at the mall or local eatery. You should lay your head down at night and feel great about your daily accomplishments and how someone is better off because of you or your product. If you're spending your nights having to scheme about how you can increase your bottom line then you will not tend to reap the rewards of *Accidental Increase*. I find that those who focus solely on making money miss out on more valuable things. Everyone in America knows the blatant example of this from the antagonist in Charles Dickens' *A Christmas Carol*. Scrooge missed feelings of accomplishment and genuine relationships that he was not even aware existed. Suffice it to say, if the blocks on the bottom of the pyramid are properly proportioned, the top will take care of itself. Money is not at the base of the pyramid folks! Money simply follows value and rarely precedes it. When you create or bring worth, money is usually the reward. It's all about reliability and value.

---

10 Strange voices calling your home around 5:30 at night during dinner.

It's easy to sell something of real value! Easy as pie. Only when a product is worth less than you claim, do you have to have a set of skills in order to sell it. Many salespeople are master deceivers. They don't believe in their product at all. They have to learn tactics and skill sets to deceive their clients. They become masters of deception. They lie, cheat and many times will steal. They inflate pricing just so they can claim they're giving you a deal when they lower it. They resort to powers of persuasion in order to manipulate their victims' intelligence.

In his book, *Influence, The Psychology of Persuasion,*[11] Dr. Robert B. Cialdini sites this amazing illustration. In the early 60's and 70's, the *Hare Krishna Society*[12] was financially floundering due to their strange appearance and unwanted solicitations around street corners and airports. But something spectacular occurred in the mid 70's that turned them into a financial empire. It was the giving of a gift. This simple gesture turned the entire organization around in a near astounding fashion. Passersby would be given several oddities, including a flower. Even if the reluctant individual refused it, the Krishna's would not take it back. What followed was a knee-jerk emotional response that we now know as the Reciprocity Principle. Because they used this tool with cunning accuracy, it was only after receiving the gift that the unsuspecting victims were asked for a donation.

The power of the emotional need to "pay-back" was so strong that the benefactor would feel compelled to make a small donation even if the flower was discarded minutes later...genius? This ultimately leaves a very bad taste in the mouths of the recipients. These people got away with giving a worthless item for the victims' hard earned wages. You see this same thing in many religious sects today. Mainline Christian television will tout some of these masters of deception...evil in my opinion. As men and women of character, you need to make sure people are better off for knowing you or your product, not ripped off!

---

11 Copyright 1984, 1993 by Robert B. Cialdini, Quill William Morrow New York
12 The International Society for Krishna Consciousness (ISKCON), also known as 'the Hare Krishna' movement, is one of the Hindu Vaishnava religious organizations. It was founded in 1966 in New York City by A.C. Bhaktivedanta Swami Prabhupada.

The Consistency Rule

Next we will discover the power of the consistency rule and how it can create an accidental increase in the lives of those who unwittingly wield its power. A pair of Canadian psychologists performed an interesting experiment that yielded some very unusual results. People who placed a bet at a racetrack, were much more confident that their particular choice of horse would win *after* placing the bet, than they were *prior* to placing the bet. It appears that once we have crossed the line by actually performing an action, we will adjust our thinking as well as our beliefs to align with the action. This is the consistency rule. This rule can work for or against us in many ways.

I do not want to delve too deep into these principles of persuasion because the main goal is to help you understand the idea of *Accidental Increase* so I will just be touching on these rules. When we act in a positive way by taking a leap of faith or risking monetary means to explore a venture that we believe will be beneficial, we will inadvertently bind the expected result to ourselves by living consistent with the expected outcome. This binding will actually *create* it. We first create it in our minds and then we create it in our actions. Yet, it will work both *for* and *against* us. To illustrate, let's pretend that you are a woman who is dating a man who is jobless and has a drinking problem.[1]

Your friends spend countless hours trying to convince you that this is not a bright idea-to keep this relationship from moving forward. Your boyfriend, however, woos you back away from your friends' logic whenever you get alone with him. Let's say this goes on for months until one day you go away on a business trip. You end up spending a week and a half with a very sensible co-worker who finally gets through to you while you and your boyfriend are apart.

You then break things off and find a more suitable candidate for a long term relationship and are finally happy that you saw the light. Your former boyfriend however, continues to call and emotionally manipulate you by pushing all your guilt buttons and by being repentant. He even promises to get a job and quit drinking. Are you getting this picture? This is far too often the case, I am afraid. Now let's say your former boyfriend wins the fight for

---

1 This illustration is purely fictional.

you and you end up conceding in a moment of utter guilt and weakness and break it off with the more suitable candidate. You have just made an incredibly important decision and therefore are going to have to live in a manner consistent with such a powerful choice. Now let's skip ahead six months and see that your boyfriend is still jobless and has decided that he can continue to drink as long as he does not have violent outbursts.

And you? You are *more* satisfied with him now than you were before you picked back up with him the second time. You make excuses for his low sense of urgency and coddle his poor performance. You even start drinking with him so that he doesn't feel alone and judged. You tell yourself rational lies in order to make your world line up with the decision you made six months earlier. The decision was to pick up with him because *he was going to get a job and stop drinking.*

Of course, he hasn't accomplished either of these goals but you don't see it that way. You now see him as consistently quitting drinking and then blame the economic condition or perhaps even the president for that matter for his lack of employment! This is all done to align yourself with the unbelievably poor decision you have made. You will not be able to admit stupidity because that takes honesty. You will not see this decision as poor judgment because that takes brains. This is because you have invested so much time and brainpower no matter how limited! You will create a false world in order to line up with the fact that he is going to quit drinking and get a job. In your mind, this is exactly what he *is doing* even if he is not. I might add this as well…*God help the person who tries to tell you otherwise!* This is an example of how the consistency rule works against us, especially against those who lack Emotional Intelligence. In my own life, I have started completely over on "purpose" 4 times in a span of 25 years. Each time I would say; "There is NO plan B" and I meant it. And you know what? There wasn't.

Social Proof

The social proof principle is just as powerful as the previous principles. Social proof is when society or perceived popularity dictates an individual's next move. I remember not long ago driving towards a very busy intersection near where I live. I was going to make a left turn and as I was approaching the light, so I noticed the arrow had turned yellow. The car in front of me arrived at the light a few seconds after it had turned red, but still continued to stroll right on through. Here's what happened next. I proceeded to follow the car without reservation and blatantly ran the red light nearly causing an accident![2] Do you see what just occurred? The car in front of me provided the social proof that it was all right to run the light. This all transpired within my mind in nanoseconds. I was stupefied and mortified that I had just run the red light (But happy because I got to my destination earlier)!

One summer day, my daughter was attending a concert on the green down by the bay near my town. The weather was dreadful and the band was apparently pretty lame as well. She told me that it was one of the most boring events she had ever attended and was beside herself with frustration because everyone was just standing around like they were attending a zombie convention.

She then started pushing her girlfriends at the front of the stage and they returned the favor. Giggling back and forth and shoving each other around apparently alerted the rest of the zombies and they had the social proof they needed to begin having fun in spite of the band's lack of talent. This turned into a frenzied mosh-pit styled avalanche of behavioral modification. The whole place erupted! My daughter ended up having a rather good time and it all started when she introduced the idea of having fun to a crowed that believed it wasn't warranted. This was of course due to the lousy band and bad weather. She provided the social proof everyone not only needed, but actually wanted.

Even though most people there lacked the courage to enact the behavior necessary to create the good time, they all enjoyed it after the social encouragement. You may be wondering how accidentally evoking the social proof principle creates *Accidental Increase*. I would pin this down to producing the proof that work is fun. A bad situation is not so bad after all. This happens accidentally by introducing the behavior that corresponds to that bright idea! You create the proof necessary for some to agree with you behaviorally. When this happens, the atmosphere around you changes. Those

---

2 I ran a stoplight at Cranberry crossing in Kingston, MA at approximately 3:10 p.m. on the 23rd of February 2008.

who do this as a way of life are what I call thermostats. Thermometers record the temperature. Thermostats regulate it. What I mean is, you are either a critic or a creator.

Looking over my life I have discovered this one truth. I am a creator. I create the environment I want and if it is not possible to do so, I leave the environment — period (Watch out honey!). I don't stick around and criticize it. This was never something I sought out to do. One day I just realized that I was doing it. I tend to bring the social proof necessary which enables others who want change to attempt to incorporate change-agents. This actually helps to bring it about. I invite people to participate in emotional and environmental changes wherever I am. This I have noticed is essential for increase.

> "I create the environment I want and if it is not possible to do so, I leave the environment."

Liking

The liking rule is simple. People tend to buy from, hang around and admire those they like, more than they do those whom they do not like. Those who experience Accidental Increase are more often than not, liked by other people. In fact, they are just flat likable. Ancient King Solomon once said that, "*A man who has friends must himself be friendly.*"[3] Here's a bit of wisdom for you. If you are a likable person, more people will like you. Sixty years of data from the behavioral corporate environment tells us that if someone likes you and you are a salesperson (influencer), then they will more than likely purchase your product as long as the product seems good. This is very telling, yet many act as if they were never told. Being likable consists of bringing value while presenting oneself as carefree and real. Likeable people are also able to find humor in the difficulties of life and they are great at caring. These attributes may sound simple, but for some, they are insurmountable. Many times salespeople will actually *pretend* to like you in

---

3 Proverbs 18:24 (NKJV)

an effort to create within you the need to buy (*You can pick these people out when you leave their presence and feel like you need to take a shower*).

Likable people tend not to rely on happiness because happiness is usually based upon favorable circumstances. They rely instead upon joy, which is independent of circumstances. Joy results from believing the unbelievable and relying on strengths greater than your own. This is why those who have a deep faith tend to endure difficulty with greater peace than those who have none.

You might say that these people are ignorant or stupid; go ahead. I would much rather be ignorant and love my life than so-called smart and hate it. People who believe that everything depends upon their own ability always hit the ceiling first. Hitting the ceiling does not promote a sense of fulfillment or happiness, but creates a negative aura that smacks of discontentment, frustration and sometimes anger.

As you might guess, these are not necessarily the ingredients for being liked by those around you. I remember when I was in seminary in the mid 80's. I was married and living in Oklahoma far from family and friends at 22 years of age. We were driving a Datsun B210 hatchback and the brakes were going bust. We were virtually penniless but were having the time of our lives. I have a particular memory that is as clear as if it were this morning. In this memory, I was thinking, "God, my car is in need of a brake job!"[4] As I think back to those times, I realize that from an early age I fully depended on strength far greater than my own when it came to things that seemed insurmountable. Therefore I was able to live a carefree life without much ceiling. This wasn't a blatant display of stupidity, but rather reliance upon one greater than me. Funny thing is, the brakes were fine soon after that![5]

OK, I am not a loon but maybe a bit loony. What I am about to tell you may seem unbelievable at first, but I assure you, it happened just as I am about to describe. My wife and I basically had no money during this time. I was attending classes from about 8 a.m. till noon five days a week. While I was at school, my wife was working about 50 hours a week including Saturdays at *Jim Nelson Ford*[6] in Broken Arrow. (I still remember your sacrifice

---

4 This took place in Tulsa, OK in 1986.
5 Another weird miracle; we're getting used to these.
6 The best job my wife ever had. The Nelson's were unbelievable human beings and still are.

honey... I love you!) I would go to work from about one in the afternoon until 11 at night. Needless to say, we saw little of each other those first few years, but when we came together...*yeah baby!*

I was jobless during this time and spent everyday after school looking for work while my poor wife worked her little heart out at the dealership. I think I can honestly say we were starving to death (exaggerating). I'm writing this while smiling because it's such a fond memory. Our rent was $210 a month, if you can believe that! After we paid it and the other bills, we had little if nothing left for food and gas. We also had only one car at the time.

Now here's the unbelievable part. I came home one day at around 3 in the afternoon after looking for work and found the kitchen refrigerator full of food! The cabinets were packed to overflowing as well. Also, typically when shopping, the cheaper way was to buy the local store brands instead of the NAME brands. These always had a yellow & black label. After we would go the grocery store the inside of our cabinets always looked as if we were being attacked by a giant yellow jacket. On this particular day however, the cabinets looked quite different. Everything was "brand-name" only!

I phoned my wife in order to find out how she pulled this off only to discover she had never left the dealership. She had only spent time in the ladies room praying by the sink at around 10 that morning. She prayed that God would feed us somehow (*As a man trying to provide for the family, this made me feel like king of the idiots*). I dare say that someone had broken into our apartment and rather than stealing our limited amount of belongings, they gave us about two weeks worth of groceries. I later found out that a gentleman by the name of Adam Boyd[7] was the culprit. I had recently met Adam at school and he was sitting behind me in class when *it happened.* He claimed that God told him to shop for my wife and I after class because we were in need of food. It was during that class that my wife was at the dealership in the bathroom asking God for help. *All I can say is she did, God did and then Adam did.*

I have since come to a conclusion that has helped me in life and believe it will help you as well. Knowing who you are *NOT* is far better than knowing who you are. I knew that under these particular circumstances I was

---

7 Adam is the best Bible teacher I have ever heard to date.

unable to accomplish much in terms of supplying our needs, being in school and all. I just couldn't dig fast enough. In other words, I sucked[8] at making money during this time in my life. My wife knew it as well. She had rightly surmised this, but went to God and stood in faith that he would supply what I lacked (*I was also praying as we did this every morning before starting the day*).

She didn't hold it against me, but rather *supported me* when it was tough going. She knew my character and I knew hers. We both knew that this was a job for Superman and we didn't feel like two losers because of it. We rejoiced in the idea of how he was going to pull it off. It was almost a game. We were weak, but he was strong. We were not the brightest bulbs on the tree, but he made the trees! We did everything in our power possible and then left the impossible to God. Adam is still my close friend and as a matter of fact, he just interrupted me with a phone call about 8 minutes ago. Bugger. Ah yes, now I remember; this all started because Adam *liked* me.

An Appeal to Authority

Have you ever wondered why we will stand in front of a man or woman wearing a white lab coat and drop our drawers nearly without hesitation? Do you know why it's so easy to do this? I'll tell you. It's all about the lab coat. The lab coat represents authority. In fact, in 2005 a 76-year-old man posed as a physician and was later arrested for going door-to-door and offering free breast exams (*He miraculously got away with 2 of them!*). His lab coat and black doctor's bag enabled unsuspecting women to believe he was a legitimate doctor — NOT! Anyone could grab a clipboard, don a hard hat and inspect a multi-million-dollar job site without being stopped because they are showing signs of authority by holding a clipboard, wearing a hard hat and boldly walking around. Those who walk in *Accidental Increase* also appeal to authority in many ways without even realizing it.

The power of the appearance of authority has very powerful ramifications and will cause others to take note when it is implemented in the right way. A 100-pound policeman with a bad hair day can stand in the middle of

8 As in sucking pond water — one of my favorite things to say and one of my least favorite things to do.

the road and stop a semi-tractor-trailer with little or no effort, all because he is wearing the correct uniform. If someone tried that wearing a T-shirt and Bermuda shorts, he might get killed. A 90 pound woman soaking wet can command you to put your seat in an upright position and move your bags no matter how big or important you think you are and you'll *obey* her (As you should). If people believe that you know what you are doing, you will command their attention even if you don't know what you are talking about.

One of my problems as a twenty something was getting found out that I really wasn't as well informed as everyone originally thought (including myself). I would speak with such authority on subjects I had just recently learned, that I would never be questioned. I wasn't trying to deceive people, I was simply quite excited about my newly learned subject. So, donning that excitement, I would launch right into it with such passion and conviction that everyone would immediately buy the idea, including me. This is typical of visionaries who tend more often than not to fly by the seat of their pants.

About a year ago, I was doing a talk that centered in on the idea of how we tend to record events as images within our mind. I had recently been learning of such things from a book that was recommended to me. I also engaged in a bit of Internet research.[9] After my 45-minute talk, an Asian gentleman approached me with a question. He assumed that I was a neurologist! He believed me to be an authority on the subject simply because of the way I presented the information - boldly and filled with zeal. I felt like I had signed up for brain class after simply reading the book and checking my facts. I loved the information and was thrilled to share it with those around me because it was extremely helpful to me. The session was very informative and helped a lot of people.

When you are passionate about something, I would suggest that you might as well be the representative of it. *It's the conviction that creates the authority.* Accuracy combined with the passion to share the information so all can reap the same harvest as you did equals increase. Those who spent even a small amount of time with the Christ would leave saying "...I have never heard anyone speak with such authority..." Why? He was passionate and he was *right* — period. If you have ever had a remarkable teacher in your past

---

9 I don't make a habit of this. This was just one of those situations… you know the drill.

that held a position of authority in your life, you can probably trace it back to their passion for the *subject* and their passion for *you*.[10] Sometimes, just knowing more than the one you are with makes you an authority, if you present your case confidently. It's not that you know everything; it's just that you know *more*. This is why being a resource is so powerful. You should always be taking in new information as a way of life. Being a resource will create *Accidental Increase* in your life and relationships because givers always gain.

The first man on earth, Adam was a *living soul* but Christ was a *life giving Spirit*.[11] Be a giver, not a taker. Understand that appearance, clothing and confidence are all automatic authority producers. When I started the consulting business in 2005, I purchased a pair of glasses to wear. This is because when I was 10 years old, I had a large nail go through my left eye. It left me legally blind in that eye (you poor dear!). Moreover, the kids I went to school with would actually punch me right on the eye patch and call me "the pirate." It would break my heart, and not do my eye much good either.

Within a year, my eye began to drift to the left. Now, 35 years later, I look like a freak! I know, I know, this is great for winning friends and influencing people! I am amazed at how self-conscious I am about this at 45 years of age. What I decided to do was to wear glasses in an attempt to turn the "cosmetic confusion" of the situation around and hopefully also deter my unsuspecting victims away from the evil vulture eye; I kid you not. It has ended up giving me authority. I know this because of what those who know me have said. They claim that I now look "distinguished," "smart" and like I know what I'm talking about. One person even told me (in jest) I should start my own religion! This is all pretty funny in one sense, but on another level, it is completely true. The way you carry yourself will determine what others perceive about what you know. As long as you are not a lying, manipulating monster, the appeal to authority will cause *Accidental Increase* in your life. By the way, the glasses I wear are simply glass, non-prescription.

Another way to receive authority by accident is to simply be responsible. Authority is the acceptance of responsibility, which is all-important. One of the biggest problems within our culture today is people want authority without the acceptance of responsibility. Responsible people always move

10 My all time favorite schoolteacher was Tony Cooke (Rhema 1985-1987).
11 1 Corinthians 15:45

up. You could say that authority is the fruit of responsibility. Responsible actions create appeals to authority. I remember cleaning up a mess one time in a particular store. An irresponsible person decided it was more important to ramble off to wherever they were going than to keep the isle neat. A customer asked me; "Do you work here?" The fact is that because I was being responsible it created the illusion that this particular outfit employed me. What do you think customers think when they see an employee dressed in uniform wasting company time? You're right - Wait until his boss sees him! You would never suspect them to *be* the boss.

When I was in high school, I would go to work with my father sometimes during the summer and we would show up on the job about 40 minutes before anyone else and just sit in the truck and wait. I thought this was ridiculous. One day I asked my father why we were there so early and he replied; *"You should always be here and ready to work before the boss gets here."*[12] No matter what my father ever did, he rose to the top while doing it in regards to *work* ethic (Not to be confused with morality). He has always worked with his hands, but for someone who works with his hands, he is an authority on the subject of construction. Everyone goes to Clarence Sisler when they need to know anything about building. I believed him that day in the truck and that began my *Accidental Increase* in the area of authority and *work* ethic.

The Scarcity Rule

You had better buy it today because by tomorrow, they might all be gone! This is the scarcity rule. Most advertisers use this tactic as a way to get you to buy. I heard of a gentleman who would buy used cars from a wholesaler and then turn around and sell them right out of his front yard. The amazing thing was that he made a small fortune doing it. Now if any of us tried that, it would probably not be as successful. When he did it, however, it was very successful and here's why. He consistently evoked the scarcity rule. He would put an ad in the local paper and wait for folks to call. But, here was the catch. He would make the same appointment for the same two or

---

12 1981 My father is a workaholic.

three people. The first person to look at the car usually purchased it for fear that the other two would buy it if they didn't. Even if they didn't really need the car or it wasn't the exact car they were looking for, they still bought it for fear of losing it!

An experiment was conducted by social psychologist Stephen Worchel.[13] What Worchel and his team accomplished was very simple. The participants in a consumer-preference study were given a chocolate-chip cookie from a large jar containing similar cookies and were asked to taste the cookie and rate its value. Half the participants were given a jar containing 10 cookies and the other half was given a jar containing just two cookies. Based upon the scarcity rule, you can probably guess what happened. When the cookie was one of the only two available, it was rated much more favorably than when rated among 10 cookies. The cookie in short supply became much more valuable in taste, appearance and monetary value than the cookie in abundant supply.

In the writings of King Solomon, we read a most amazing bit of wisdom; *"Seldom set foot in your neighbor's house — too much of you, and he will hate you."*[14] Solomon in all his wisdom knew that as a friend, it is better to be scarce than consistently in the face of another, especially when that person is in trouble. Knowing when to leave creates *Accidental Increase* in your life. When you are in short supply, your advice and whatever else you have to offer becomes much more valuable than when you don't have the EQ[15] to know exactly when to leave or shut up. What we need to understand is that part of being valuable is being scarce. Just like diamonds or rubies, it's the scarcity that creates the value. It took me years to learn how to be quiet. I have a couple of conditions working against me. The first is adult ADHD[16] and the second is an insatiable need to be liked by everyone. (*This was a whole lot worse about 10 years ago and since then has been completely reversed.*) People like me tend to gush from the mouth simply because there's nothing else to

13 Worchel, S., J. Lee, and Adewole. "The Effects of Supply and Demand on Ratings of Object value." *Journal of Personality and Social Psychology* 32 (1975) 906-14).

14 Proverbs 25:17

15 The ability to manage your emotions in order to benefit all involved is the Emotional Quotient.

16 Attention Deficit Hyperactive Disorder — my best friend.

do. After reading from Solomon's school of the wise (Proverbs), I learned that *"even a fool is thought wise if he keeps silent...."*[17]

The Power of Caring

The power of caring is simple. The more you focus your attention on the needs of other people, the better off you become. This is not compulsive care giving. That's dysfunctional. This is a healthy caring with healthy boundaries. Caring is an art. Caring is about having proper regard for other people, to be concerned or solicitous. Finally, this is about being watchful or making conscientious efforts to do something exactly right for another person. The difficulty today is finding someone who doesn't have an angle. Your telephone rings around 5 p.m. and a joyous voice interrupts your meal with a hearty, "Hello, how are you this evening?" Your first thought is completely negative and you feel positioned to be taken advantage of. This is because many use the rules of persuasion and acts of kindness in order to relax you into a state of vulnerability and then, when you least expect it, they rob you blind. Don't ever allow this behavior to stop you from doing what is just, fair and right.

You cannot let another's poor performance regulate yours. It's time you begin to use the power of care against the tide! Though many manipulators abound, keep caring! The late Mother Teresa[18] instructed us to care even when others don't and to love even when others don't. Those who care naturally will then by default experience *Accidental Increase* in their lives. Some people find caring as a weary endeavor and some just like existing alone (*Being alone can be a blessing, but being lonely is a curse*). I suggest always finding some time to care for others in your week and you will be far better off for doing it. If you haven't noticed, the art of caring is becoming a lost art within our modern society. It's this caring piece that creates the human bonds necessary to create the synergies that ultimately produce great outcomes. Everyone already knows what he or she doesn't want someone to do to him or her. It's known as The Golden Rule.

---

17 Proverbs 17:28
18 For over 45 years she ministered to the poor, sick, orphaned, and dying, while guiding the Missionaries of Charity's expansion, first throughout India and then in other countries. A freak of nature.

Solomon says that, "*The righteous care about justice for the poor, but the wicked have no such concern.*"[19] The power of caring is all about righting the injustices of this world. Those who tend towards a high individualistic attitude in life and who sport a high traditional background, tend towards righting all wrongs within their personal scope of ability. This in no way falls under the category of compulsive care giving, but rather the general concern for justice and equality where it is due. People who respond to injustice by nature will increase not only in their own lives, but they will also attract others like a magnet others who are in need of such an equalizing agent. This brings us back to the point of living the inconvenient life. As a professional profiler and behavioral analyst, I consistently deal with business leaders who lack these caring abilities and those who retain them. I have been amazed in my findings.

The leaders who embody the ability to have sincere concern for others consistently create a better team environment while those who do not tend to produce arenas where dysfunctions abound. Selfless living always produces great results in the end. One could argue that it is only the nurse who fully embodies the art of caring and that otherwise it has become a past time notion.

Caring was once seen as a weakness. Within the health profession, nurses were consistently looked down upon because the doctors were busy diagnosing and curing their patients. They were too busy to spend the necessary time by the bedside. Statistics show that quiet caring conversation by the bedside will actually lower one's blood pressure, not to mention lowering cholesterol levels in some cases. Is it any wonder why they call it health-care? It is solely because on the root level, caring produces greater health. This is the power of ethos at work. It is the power to create a sense of purpose in another person because you care enough to indulge in the life of that person and create in them the desire to live up to your expectations of them.

This is what the late Ronald Reagan[20] was able to do with ease. If you are familiar with his "tear down this wall" speech, you can read how he spoke into the heart of communists and simply called them up to a higher standard. He did not spend time making them feel like they were evil. He believed in

---

19 Proverbs 29:7
20 Ronald Wilson Reagan (February 6, 1911 — June 5, 2004) was the 40th President of the United States.

them more than they believed in themselves and his caring for them was also quite evident. This begs the question, what did Ronald Reagan's caring do for such a people? The answer is summed up in one of the greatest photos of the 21st century. In the photograph, Mikhail Gorbachev, the former leader of the communist regime stares as if hopeless, with one hand resting upon the coffin of the deceased Reagan.

4

Ulterior Motivation

The Power of Selfless Living

"It is easy to love the people far away. It is not always easy to love those close to us. It is easier to give a cup of rice to relieve hunger than to relieve the loneliness and pain of someone unloved in our own home. Bring love into your home for this is where our love for each other must start."

—MOTHER TERESA

Selfless Living

Ulterior motives. They are generally agenda driven ideas that result in a selfish approach to building one's personal wealth or reputation. However, when I speak of ulterior motives, I am referring to something opposite of the definition listed above. If you look at the cultural norms of advancement, you may notice that folks who gain momentum often do so by cheating others or by doing things that are downright squirrely. Accidental Increase, on the other hand, produces those who succeed when success isn't even the goal. In his wisdom literature, Solomon writes about those who consistently cast their bread upon the water.[1] Over time, he suggests that they will end up seeing it return upon the waves against the shoreline. Do you understand? Over the years, I have come to realize that the secret of those who increase is their philosophy of generosity. The results are astounding. Those who give much, receive more. I know this seems backwards, but I assure you otherwise.

Thanksgiving 1988. My wife and I were seated at our little card table in the kitchen of our small apartment in Massachusetts. We were in need of several hundred dollars for something that I find hard to recall at the moment. What is easier to recall was how we acquired the money for this important item. Remember I previously wrote about Adam-the friend who bought us the food in Oklahoma? Well, Adam's uncle Jeff[2] had realized some extra money through a project he was working on in Georgia. He sent this extra money to a charity. Then while Uncle Jeff was talking to God one day he felt like God spoke to him during his prayer.

My wife and I received a check in the mail (from Uncle Jeff) for somewhere around $600. He had called the charitable organization and requested the money back so he could send it to us! He claimed that God told him he had mistakenly sent it to the wrong party and that he needed to get it back and send it to us instead. Of course, the truly amazing aspect of this story is that he actually did it!

This in fact, has been our story for 25 years! We do our best to live selflessly, and find a consistency in moving forward through miraculous ways. I have found these principles as steady as gravity. Am I guaranteeing that everyone who lives selflessly will receive checks in the mail? Yes, absolutely. But that's not the point! The motivation of those who Accidentally Increase, is not to get "paid." When you depend upon God for your needs, treat people as you want to be treated and believe what God says is actually true, you will experience the miracle. My parents have not only taught me these truths, but have lived by these truths in regards to giving and have given away eight cars to prove it. In 1979 when we were scheduled to move to Florida from Massachusetts, my older brother totaled the family car by accident. OK, call it accidental decrease! Within about a week's time, a Swedish gentleman in his

---

1 Ecclesiastes 11:1-6
2 Uncle Jeff is hilarious, a risk taker and an all around freak fpr justice.

late 60s (who knew my parents) handed my father the keys to a brand new car. *His* brand new car! When he heard about our misfortune, God supplied it, through the man. This car was only a few months old!

Need more evidence? Around the same period of time, my parents were short about $1000. This was the rest of the money our family needed to move to Florida. While fishing at a local pond, my dad actually caught an old antique jewelry box. It ended up containing a few 24 carat gold necklaces! He was able to sell those for around $1000. I know this sounds like a "fish story" but I promise it's all true.[3] Over the years, I've watched as my parents kept the momentum of increase going (When it came to giving) more often than not. Is it any wonder that I have assumed the same position in my own life?

The "You First" Axiom

The "you first" axiom is something I identified recently. It asserts the act of putting yourself in an appropriate position when dealing with people in any and all circumstances. The way this works is YOU always consider the other person superior to yourself and therefore become second to them. I gleaned this little nugget from St. Paul's idea of *"esteeming others better than yourself."*[4] Now remember, this isn't a tactic or trick for gaining, but rather a life principle that is lived out for better or worse. These are not formulas for success, but rather principles for living regardless of the outcome. It has only been by looking back over my life that I've begun to discover how these things have played out and to be quite honest, I can't even guarantee their future continuation.

Esteeming others is not simply an idea, but is more of a compulsory act based upon my understanding of Christ's teachings. My desire is to please him. After all, he loved me first.[5] My wholesome dread of displeasing him is where this begins. Living his way transpires from a relationship of trust that has been built over time. Consider your own family, for a minute. Now consider the anxiety of displeasing your dad or mom. What does this anxiety

---

3 This is a modern version of the miracle of the coin in the fish as recorded in Matthew 17:27.
4 Philippians 2:3
5 I John 4:19

Recognizing is the cornerstone of responsibility. It's when we recognize that we are not fulfilling our obligations that we become increasingly responsible in changing our behavior

produce in you? Does it produce a compulsion to do what pleases him/her or does it produce rebellion in you? In other words, do you desire to act in concert or in contradiction to their wishes? Relationship becomes the cornerstone of correctness. "You first" principled people generally build relationships with others that allow them to say "No" once in awhile, and still be received as friend not foe.

Rules without relationship lead to rebellion nearly every time. It is only when you have a healthy relationship with your father that you can assemble the desire to please him for all the right reasons. This paradigm is a pleasure principle that seeks to please others rather than self. It doesn't mean that we don't fall short now and again. What it does mean is that we are consistently striving for excellence but we can also recognize when we are not walking in it. Recognizing is the cornerstone of responsibility. It's when we recognize that we are not fulfilling our obligations that we become increasingly responsible in changing our behavior. It's when we fail to realize our shortfalls that we fail to increase in this life.

When your *"wholesome dread is displeasing your heavenly father,"*[6] it causes you to instinctively act in line with what you believe would be pleasing to him. Some people may have had earthly fathers who did not look out for their personal welfare, or who violated trusts, confidences or sexual boundaries. Sadly, this is becoming far too common today. My heart aches for such people. Seeking to please one's father who violated such natural laws often causes very negative knee-jerk reactions from these poor suffering souls. But I must warn you; this can create an unhealthy desire to win one's favor at the expense of one's emotions. It also can negatively affect one's physical health. You are priceless and loved no matter what happened to you during your formative years. It is not your fault, and I understand you can't just get over

6 I heard my college professor Doug Jones say this phrase in 1986 at Rhema Bible Training Center.

it. Wounds that run deeply always require a much longer grieving process. I hope that you will search and find the support of those who are willing to help you take the lid off of these awful memories and begin the process of restoration. You deserve this! And, your consent to open the closet could be the first step in a healthier lifestyle and a more stable emotional environment.

Always remember this- if you are breathing, then this is the vital sign that qualifies you. Simply put, YOU are precious and valuable in the sight of God. Though people will let you down, God has his eye fixed on you. Even more so, when you are in trouble! Regardless of what anyone has ever told you, God loves you. It has been through a careful examination of my own life that I have begun to discover how this "you first" principle works. I can't put a positive guarantee on every future, but I can say that you will make quite a positive difference in this world by putting this axiom to work for the good of others!

When Having Fun is the Goal

Having fun not only results in greater health both physically and mentally, but appears to be paramount in the process of Accidental Increase as well. I have always tried to make the best of all situations in life and as a result, I have consistently increased over the years. Attitude is a large part of our success or failure, yet we don't seem to realize it enough to make the proper adjustments when necessary. My daughter backed into the fire hydrant at the end of our driveway while driving my new car the other day and basically pulled half of the rear bumper off. When my wife walked in to inform me of the mishap, in a split second I knew I had to choose the proper attitude. I realized that nothing I said or did would repair the damage already done to the car, but by saying or doing the wrong thing I could easily damage my daughter's spirit.

I had to ask myself, did she do this on purpose? Was my daughter aiming for the hydrant in an evil attempt to destroy my property? Or was she simply a bit hasty getting out of the driveway? I walked calmly onto the driveway and assessed the damage. I proceeded to inform my daughter in jest that she was costing me a lot of money. This was the second incident as she previously tore the front bumper off in the last snowstorm. I donned my auto mechanics helmet and rebuilt humpty dumpty as much as I could. I told her to be careful and calmly made my way back into the house. It was later that my wife and I discussed in private how we would deal with the damages and whether or not my daughter would contribute some money to the cause. Realizing that it was only a car and that its importance is getting you from point A to point B was what enabled me to be calm and understanding. Placing a priority on people above objects contributes to the avoidance of unnecessary upheavals within society. Drawing the distinction between people and objects becomes part of the doorway to Accidental Increase.

I remember distinctly when my daughter was around 8 years old and taking horseback riding lessons weekly at a local barn. We began to notice that she was rather good at it. Thus began a 9-year adventure that eventually resulted in her becoming the grand champion in dressage in 2002! Early on in her riding experience she was thrown from her horse and consequently became discouraged and fearful. She came home in tears and asked me if she could quit. We had already spent hundreds of dollars on clothing and lessons at this point. My internal initial reaction was a resounding, "…are you crazy in the head? Do you know what this has cost your mother and I?"

I had to ask myself, why were we doing this? Was it for the simple fact that my daughter had fun riding horses? Was it an outlet for her to grow and mature into a confident woman who could feel encouraged about her amazing accomplishments? Or, was I investing into something far more sinister — my own ego and personal well-being? If fun was the goal, how was I going to handle her being discouraged, afraid and hurt? I remember sitting down with her and asking her questions about her fall and what she was thinking about the whole ordeal. She informed me that she was no longer interested in riding. I decided to try and teach her a lesson involving the science of glue. I asked her to explain what glue was and ultimately how one would go about testing its ability to hold things together. She gave me all the right answers; glue sticks things together and the way you would test it is to try to pull things apart after gluing them.

"Hannah, you are the glue and Arashana is testing you in order to see how strong your glue is," I informed her after much deliberation. "You are a gifted rider and Arashana is feeling her oats right now. Let me tell you what

I think... I think you are the strongest glue on the planet, but that is not my decision to make, it is yours. I will stand behind your decision to give up, but I won't agree with it because I believe better of you. So you decide what you think you should do." I then kissed her on the head and left the room. The very next week, Hannah went back to the barn and Arashana subsequently tried to throw her again. According to Hannah's instructor, "she nearly jerked the horses head off" and Arashana never tried that tactic again. I told Hannah how proud I was of her and that I thought she was a great kid. Hannah looked down and then up again and with her sweet little voice said, "No, I have a great dad."

These are the moments when we come to a crossroad where we can choose ruin or restoration in our children's lives — or anyone's life for that matter. What are the goals — fun, excitement and personal growth? Or are you so bent on developing your own reputation that you steal the fun and joy from others in a feeble attempt to gain another minute of self-gratification? Life should be fun and your children should be having fun as long as you play your part. My eldest son wanted to play football with the town team one year when he was younger. After dealing with the financial obligation of $400 for the team uniform and the town remuneration, Kohen leapt onto the field with wild expectation. We soon discovered that the coaches were mini Hitler's.

"I thought this was going to be fun," my son said after one grueling practice. Yet he continued trying with all his might. He was the last child running laps around the entire field in full regalia, limping on one foot while the coaches balked and scorned him. I was ready to purchase a shotgun! I remember after one particularly brutal practice, placing my hands on his shoulders, looking him in the eye and softly saying, "you don't have to do this Kohen, maybe you're just not wired for this sort of thing."

"But you spent all that money," he replied. "It's okay sweetheart, this is about you," I said. At 16, my son now enjoys piano, golf and bodybuilding. He's having fun. Never use your children to accomplish your failed dreams. Help them build their own.

Balance is the Key to Life

The late Dr. Edwin Louis Cole made a statement in the mid 1980's that I will not soon forget. He said, "Balance is the key to life." We live by balancing carbon dioxide and oxygen. We live by balancing positives and negatives. These are things we can't do without. Take a car battery for instance. It utilizes the power of both positive and negative energy. This harnessed, focused power creates the flow of electricity, which drives the car, lights the road, and plays the radio. These are all good things even though they have a negative polarity attached to them at inception. Part of Accidental Increase is the ability to properly balance work and family, drive and relaxation, sense and nonsense. The ability to do this without thought can be even more rewarding.

I love to work and love working really hard and thus part of my success can be attributed to just knowing when to go home. I adopted a saying several years ago — "I work to live as opposed to living to work." I went into business for myself 20 years ago because I wanted to be home more than I wanted to be away. This one life change has led to many significant and positive differences along the way. Adding another dimension to this model — the Spiritual dimension, completes the wheel of fortune. In my experience, the balance between the personal/domestic, the societal/work and the spiritual/cause realms' is critical to increase. It's when our personal life, domestic life and spiritual life are all simultaneously firing at top performance that we reach peak levels of increase.

"By contrast, children who eat dinner with their families every night of the week are 20 percent less likely to drink, smoke, or use illegal drugs."

I take time for personal reflection as a matter of standard course in my life and always have. This keeps me in check with who I really am. Spending ample family time has also been a powerful mechanism for personal growth. We have had dinner together as a family every night for 25 years. According to a 2002 CASA[7] Teen Survey, children who do not eat dinner with their families are 61 percent more

---

7 The National Center on Addiction and Substance Abuse.

likely to use alcohol, tobacco, or illegal drugs. By contrast, children who eat dinner with their families every night of the week are 20 percent less likely to drink, smoke, or use illegal drugs. Teens who eat frequent family dinners are less likely than other teens to have sex at young ages, get into fights, or be suspended from school. They even have less thoughts of suicide! I grew up in a home where family mealtime was the highlight of the day. This gives new meaning to the idea of having a balanced meal doesn't it?

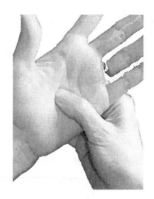

5

Cardiac Alignment

The Power of The Middle

"How true Daddy's words were when he said: all children must look after their own upbringing. Parents can only give good advice or put them on the right paths, but the final forming of a person's character lies in their own hands."

— ANNE FRANK

The Human Spirit

We as humans are spirit, soul and body. Part of the process of Accidental Increase is not only understanding how each piece fits, but also understanding the nature of the interaction between these three components. As we move through this chapter, my intention is to fully disclose the information regarding each part. I also want to help you discover how to live within the middle of your own life. As you have probably noticed by now, I live out of a biblical worldview and I don't apologize for that. Let me also be clear - this is not a personal philosophy, but rather it is more of a relationship I have developed with God through Christ. Before we proceed further, I want to share some personal reflections.

In my opinion, the spirit inside us is probably the most neglected of the three components. It is easy for people to focus on being healthy and physically fit. This seems to pretty naturally for most of us. We also believe in sharpening our learning skills for better human interaction, and engaging in the science of discovery. That said, how much time do we devote to building up the person on the inside? Not only that, but who is in there to begin with? These are very important questions that at least deserve their day in court. I will begin by telling you that the spirit is the place of intension. By "intension" I mean that it is the place of knowing, believing and being.

When we say that someone is in good spirits, what are we actually saying? We are speaking of one's attitude. The attitude always reflects the spirit within. There's an account in the gospel narratives where a couple of followers of Jesus make a suggestion. They propose burning the Samaritan evildoers to a crisp! To this Jesus replies, *"You do not know what manner of spirit you are of."*[1] Or, in our modern vernacular, *"get a hold of yourselves, you morons."*

Spiritual adjustments always lead to attitude adjustments and typically I find that you can't have the one without the other. Those who tend to be on top of this will experience Accidental Increase with better ease. You are a spirit, you have a soul and you live in a body. We are spiritual beings and our spirit is conceived at conception, just like the body. This is helpful to consider when understanding what it means to live in the middle of your life.

The human spirit is the part of us that *"knows,"* and it takes faith to rely upon its' voice. Yet again, our tendency is to concentrate on improving our earthly house or tent (the body). It should come as no surprise that everything this world throws our way is geared towards external improvements.

Do you believe that with enough time and money, doctors could create a perfect you? No matter how many surgeries Michael Jackson had on his nose, it still wasn't good enough. We all have the same sentence hanging over us. We will grow old, and move into eternity. People who are older and wiser seem to have a paradigm shift. They start out young and full of vigor, driven to succeed. Yet, as life moves on, they begin to ask themselves, "What has

---

1 Luke 9:55 (NKJV)

been my significance in this world? How have I made a difference?" They move from a place of performance to a place of maturity. Your spirit should be your utmost concern! Don't bother spending so much time on the tent that you "dwell" in. Isn't it funny how things can get turned upside down so quickly? According to the masses, the way to gain is to take what you can; yet according to Jesus, gaining comes from your ability to let things go.

"Spiritual adjustments always lead to attitude adjustments and typically I find that you can't have the one without the other."

Many believe that being "spiritual" is nothing more than being weird. Why dwell on such subjective ideas of obscure nonsense, they reason. The truth is that spiritual understanding begins with the acknowledgement of your creator.[2] This is the last place many people want to begin, because it means that there indeed is a truth. It means that there is right and wrong. It means that we need to take responsibility for our actions and beliefs. It means we have to land the plane! I find that modern day spirituality has become a hodgepodge of relativistic notions that boil down to one philosophy, one ideology and one theology — *Nobody's going to tell me what to do!*

You will never increase properly in this life until you first let go of the notion that you are the boss.

The Human Soul

The most important part of the spirit/soul dynamic is this; they cannot be separated, they can only be distinguished.[3] The interrelationship between the human will and intellect is apparently beyond the quantum level. I spent the better part of seven years studying these concepts during the 1980's and have found that these human characteristics play a far greater role than many of us want to admit. Whereas the spirit of man tends to be

---

2 Proverbs 1:7
3 Hebrews 4:12 - show us how these two can be distinguished yet not separated because they are the qualities of the "one" heart.

"When your spirit is in "shape," or more importantly, when you are "clear" in conscience, the reliability of its voice becomes increasingly more apparent."

the "knower," the soul of man tends to be the "feeler." The emotions, the intellect, and the "deep thought" are all aspects of the soul. In psychoanalysis and other forms of depth psychology, the psyche (sī-kē) refers to the forces in an individual that influence thought, behavior and personality. The word is borrowed from the ancient Greek language and refers to the concept of the self, encompassing the modern ideas of soul, self, and mind interchangeably. The Greeks believed that the soul or "psyche" was responsible for behavior.

The soul is frequently responsible for our mood and can be extremely deceptive. Feelings lie. They not only lie, but they are capable of misinterpreting very important emotions. The spirit is often a better barometer for the way things really are. When your spirit is in "shape," or more importantly, when you are "clear" in conscience, the reliability of its voice becomes increasingly more apparent.

Based upon Christian doctrine as handed down through the centuries, I am of the very strong opinion that your spirit can be regenerated or reborn through the Spirit of Christ. When this rebirth occurs, there is an awakening to the voice of God within you that becomes a very reliable source of both encouragement and direction. Prior to this, you will tend to be sensitive to that which is culturally acceptable or "expected" by the majority of those in your community. This is regardless of the moral impact on society or any particular individual.

After regeneration, an individual will become sensitive to the voice of reasonability that derives from a much higher authority. Often times this voice will trump the other voices regardless of how acceptable they may sound. For instance, did you know that many communities throughout history have found the sacrifice of children acceptable? The killing of innocent children upon alters was neither distasteful nor considered unethical by those engaging in such activities. The ancient city of Carthage was notorious for child sacrifice. Plutarch (ca. 46–120 AD) mentions the practice, as do Tertullian, Orosius and Diodorus Siculus. The Bible also speaks of what appears to be child sacrifice offerings at a place called the *Tophet* (literally "roasting place"). What a disgusting thought! The Canaanites, the ancestors of the Carthaginians and some Israelites even took part in this detestable practice.

Our culture has many strong voices when it comes to what is and what is not acceptable behavior. These voices will surely change with time, as do the seasons of the year. The voice of God's Spirit within us, however, will raise up a standard against these ever-changing voices. He will establish a new benchmark for behavior regardless of society's pull. Those who listen to the voice of God and act accordingly tend to move forward with a far greater *impact* than those who don't. This voice alone creates the conviction piece that we spoke of in the first section of this book.

> "Those who listen to the voice of God and act accordingly tend to move forward with a far greater *impact* than those who don't."

Crouching Tiger, Hidden Dragon

"Adam lay with his wife Eve, and she became pregnant and gave birth to Cain… later she gave birth to his brother, Abel. Now Abel kept the flocks, and Cain worked the soil. In the course of time Cain brought some of the fruits of the soil as an offering to the Lord. But Abel brought fat portions from some of the firstborn of his flock. The Lord looked with favor on Abel and his offering, but on Cain and his offering he did not look with favor. So Cain was very angry and his face was downcast. Then the Lord said to Cain, "Why are you angry? Why is your face downcast? If you do what is right, will you not be accepted? But if you do not do what is right, sin is crouching at your door, it desires to have you, but you must master it." Gen 4:1-7

Do you hear it? If you listen carefully, you might detect the faint breath of the tiger that lurks in the inner cave of your mind and heart. Soul is crouching at your door. All along, it is trying to undo what your spirit tells you. When we are moved by our soul, we are motivated by the feelings that accompany acceptable norms and methods of society. These tend to be personal ego driven notions as opposed to concepts that declare God's goodness and glory.

Ideas of the soul penetrate us like fiery darts! They want us to yield our wills, promising the fruits of pleasure and the rewards of wealth and fame. Ignorance is bliss. Like a fine piece of steak chewed and swallowed, our soul proclaims that it knows what is best for us. The tiger that crouches reveals its' deadly intention to snatch and stomp the life out of us! If we are not on guard, it drags us into the abyss where the hidden dragon dwells. Soulish living creates a "me first" mentality that exponentially increases your chances of becoming a walking shell, devoid of heavens' grace. The soul makes selfish statements like, "I don't feel like I love you anymore," or "I don't think we can afford to help them out…" You get the picture.

In contrast, your God given spirit produces a voice that says, *"Trust me. I know you think giving this money is a stupid move, but I own the cattle on a thousand hills…I'll take care of you…"*[4]

The Human Heart

"The heart is deceitful above all things and beyond cure. Who can understand it? I the Lord search the heart and examine the mind, to reward a man according to his conduct, according to what his deeds deserve." Jer. 17:9-10

What an indictment on the human condition! Fundamentally, I believe the heart consists of both spirit and soul. Although invisible, these two living parts combine to form the basis of human interaction. Yet these two factions are at war with each other. Like gladiators in the great coliseum, it is the soul verses the spirit on the playing field of our hearts. Press the "scene select" and we can vividly remember the times that we did what we shouldn't have done, and didn't do what we should have done. Think of your spirit as the *want to do good* part and your soul as the *do I have the time to do good* part.

So which one are you feeding the most? The gladiator that is well nourished will generally win the day. Those who unplug from responsibility in favor of eating bonbons are feeding the gladiator of soul. Those who Ac-

4 Psalm 50:10

cidentally Increase find a way to faithfully feed the gladiator of spirit. This is the only place where accidents don't happen. We must read the Bible earnestly, taking the time to mine the words that are sweeter than honey and more precious than gold.

This scheme is intentional. It is a battle plan for winning the ancient war against soul. David had the heart after God. Though he was known as a king, we can read the Psalms, which illustrate his great investment in friendship with his Lord. Soul still won out sometimes, but in the end David dealt with his shortcomings by dealing directly with God. Those who increase always choose God in the end, and he rewards the effort.

Living in The Middle

L iving out of your middle requires first knowing the middle exists. People of increase tend to think with their heart and follow it to the end no matter the consequence. Let me reiterate; Do not think of increase as increase of wealth or sustenance, but rather a life filled with hope, joy and pure expectation regardless of your monetary standing. In 1997 I was offered a job, which involved painting 127 stores throughout the Central/South Florida region. I turned it down because I believed in my *heart* that I was supposed to move to Massachusetts where I would be completely jobless with my wife and three children and no money in the bank. Smart move? No, it was a *heart* move - there's a big difference.

Looking back over the last 11 years, it now appears to be the smartest move I could have ever endeavored to make. Often it takes years for heart moves to translate into smart moves because you have to deal with all the well-meaning people in your life who tend to translate your behaviors through their own personal middles. This is the toughest part of being true to your own heart and living from it with resolution. We are all ultimately responsible to follow our own hearts, and the trustworthiness of its voice depends on whom or what you allow to speak into it for prolonged periods of time.

What are you filling your middle with? I remember years ago going to see a movie and about halfway through it feeling like I just swallowed a gallon of mud. I got up and left. Being resolute and true to your heart will create tremendous increase in your life. Does this mean we act perfect or never have an occasion to mess this process up? Absolutely not! This is a life long practice where we continue to forge ahead leaving no time for meaningless regret. Remember, it's not wrong to be wrong, it's wrong to stay wrong.

I have found that perhaps the most difficult part of living in the middle is the inability of your soul to trust your spirit. Your soul, left unchecked, will scheme and manipulate yourself and others at a moments notice. This is the sad truth my friends. Learning the ways of the soul thus becomes synonymous with winning the battle of the mind and the heart. St. Paul accurately remarked that the flesh and the spirit lust against one another, meaning that they are at continuous odds with each other.[5]

You may be familiar with the Genesis narrative concerning the story of Lot[6] (Abraham's nephew). St. Peter also mentions him, albeit with a pretty interesting twist. He speaks about Lot pitching his tent in the direction of Sodom. This was the first stupid move he made. The second was when he moved to town and became vexed in his eternal soul. Peter says that God had to send Abraham to rescue Lot from the detestable city. This happened because Lot had become, in essence, soul washed by the city's incessant lawlessness.

Peter says that Lot was tormented in his righteous soul from living among Sodom's evil inhabitants day after day and witnessing their wicked deeds through both his eyes and ears (the windows to the soul). His soul had become corrupted through the constant wearing down of his inner voice.

Lot's soul and his flesh finally conspired against his spirit and he needed rescue because he no longer had any rule over his own personal behavior. Solomon says that the person who cannot rule over his own spirit is like a city without walls.[7] You are out of control at that point and subject to the control of any passing army. Do you understand this? You are no longer calling the shots; the addiction is calling them now! Part of living in the middle is learning how to scold your own soul. Keeping it in line. Taking control of you for once. People of Accidental Increase always listen for signs of trouble in progress and then do something about it. Fools rush headlong

---

5 Galations 5:17
6 Genesis 14 this guy was an idiot.
7 Proverbs 25:28

and crash whereas the wise see the danger afar off and run for they're foolish lives, without respect for their reputations. Sometimes the only difference between wise and stupid is walking. People of increase are on a walk-a-thon away from stupid things.

If you can win your battles on the inside first, it will be rare that they ever make it to the outside. St. Paul noted that if you have your soul (mind) set upon the things that are spiritual, you would be spiritual. In other words, you will reap the benefits of making spiritual decisions (Godly choices). But, if you have your soul set on what the natural man (flesh) desires, you will be carnal - without the benefits of Godly decision making. This is no way to live. It's disastrous at its worst, and boring at its best. Living out of your middle is far more productive, interesting and fun. And by the way, about four months after moving to Massachusetts in 1997, the painting job I had turned down completely fell through. My heart didn't lie!

6

The Art of the Draft

The Power of Appointment

"One night I walked home very late and fell asleep in somebody's satellite dish. My dreams were showing up on TV's all over the world."
— STEVEN WRIGHT

God Does Not Take Volunteers

God does not take volunteers — *he drafts*. Anyone vaguely familiar with Bible history will tell you that God always raises a man or woman at an appointed hour, for an appointed task. We don't choose the task or the appointment, God does. *"You did not choose me, but I chose you and appointed you..."* Jesus' words to his disciples.[1] This is a very interesting conundrum. Our society is quite taken these days with noble notions of volunteerism. Here is the problem I find with volunteerism when reading the Bible. In all of salvation history, which covers the biblical narratives from the opening of Genesis to the close of the Acts, I can't find any examples of those who *"volunteered"* in the great events of the Bible.

---

1 John 15:16

Let's look at the story of Moses[2], for instance. In the book of Exodus, we find that his early years start with an ominous gesture. Pharaoh has put a death sentence on his head, along with all other Hebrew boy babies. Yet God delivered Moses via a simple papyrus basket cruise down the Nile into Pharaoh's daughter's waiting arms. Why did he survive while so many others perished? Certainly not because baby Moses stepped over some imaginary line to volunteer his services.

As Moses grew older, he was informed of his Hebrew heritage and in a moment of fury, he killed an Egyptian officer for beating a Hebrew brother. Once discovered, he fled for his life because Pharaoh put a second death sentence on his head. Where does Moses end up? He ends up in the town of Midian, hanging around with the "*sheeps*"[3]. In fact, he spends the next 40 years just minding his own business while he minds his father-in-law's flock. He resides in the town of Midian for some 40 years. Then, with the flash of a burning bush, God suddenly gets Moses' attention! Notice that Moses doesn't volunteer, but is rather reluctantly and precisely, drafted for Gods' fantastical journey.

Yes, Uncle Sam (God) drafts Moses (a human) for the weirdest military campaign ever and Moses wants no part of it. Why? Moses does not have the ability to see himself as God sees him. Look at what he says, "*Who am I, that I should go to Pharaoh and bring the Israelites out of Egypt?*"[4] I don't care whether you believe the story or not, just look at the plot. This is a great example of Accidental Increase in Moses' life. Don't be like the *sheeps*! Frame the picture or remain on stupid pills.

Unfortunately many of us see ourselves as the perfect man or woman for the job. Look at the U.S. presidential campaign process for example. All the candidates believe the nation will only function properly with themselves at the helm. Once they've had their hand at it for a couple of months, most law-abiding citizens wonder if they elected the right person. Why haven't we figured this out yet? Sometimes it's like *Gilligan's* Island in this country! We can build washing machines out of coconuts and run an entire plumbing system across our island but we can't figure out how to build a boat!

---

2 One of the meekest men on the face of the earth during his lifetime.
3 Very stupid fuzzy balls with legs. I do love saying "sheeps" though!
4 Exodus 3:11

If it was your job to pick the president of the United States, who would you select? The guy at work who's a closet genius and always gives the right advice without all the fanfare? Your brilliant nephew who hasn't figured out how smart he really is yet? Maybe you'd pick your neighbor or your best friend's father. Do you see what I'm getting at?

Some of the greatest people in the world are obscure. They always have been and God has always been a genius at digging them up. We've already looked at King David. Peter, James, John, Daniel, Amos for heaven's sake? Albert Einstein, the patent clerk? Stephen Hawking[5] who can barely blink his eyes? Now think of all those who claimed they could fix the world if we would just vote them into office and give them the chance. That's the problem with volunteers. Sometimes they get in the way of those who actually have the ability.

Bible Jerks

One of the most intriguing biblical concepts I have grappled with is why it seems some of the most productive people were also some of the most gigantic jerks on earth! When I say productive, I mean those who played a pivotal role in enabling the freakish plan of God to come to pass. Let's look at Peter in the New Testament. Although drafted, this guy was a real nitwit. He had a very big mouth and a large ego to match. Sure there are many things that Peter did right — proclaiming Jesus to be the "Son of God" for example. Then there are all the things he did wrong-advising Jesus not to go to Jerusalem, and denying Christ three times, for instance.

Sometimes we forget that this was all a preparation for his final successes at the end of his life. Peter ultimately was crucified upside-down, considering himself unworthy to die the same death as his Lord. There's a rather obscure Psalm[6] in the poetry section of the Bible that says God gave *gifts* (amazing ability or talent) to men and women, even to the rebellious. When God chooses an individual, they never seem to match our litmus test. This is because we are all idiots sometimes. Fortunately God always has an idiot-proof plan.

---

5 (Born 8 January 1942) is a British theoretical physicist; an amazing freak of nature.
6 Psalm 68:18; cross reference with Ephesians 4:7-14... weird and amazing.

"Part of *Accidental Increase* is realizing that you are *not* perfect and then coming to terms with it in a most glorious fashion."

As long as we believe that we are intelligent and have brilliant ideas about what is correct and germane to earth's weird problems, we will continue to reveal just how ridiculous and dense we actually are. That being said, I would never think of choosing someone I perceive as a jerk to do any of God's bidding, which is why I try to keep my mouth shut. Paul realized that God chooses the foolish things to debunk what we believe to be wisdom. The weak things, the despised things and the things that "are not," God uses to bring to nothing everything that we thought "was!"[7] God can do more with what he calls foolishness than we can with worldly wisdom. He is a Genius!

Have you ever been stuck in a particular dilemma when suddenly your teenage son asks you the dumbest question imaginable? Like a gem hidden among stones his rudimentary inquiry resolves your ridiculous problem. God apparently knows beforehand that people who don't look like much have all the answers. He hand picks them and uses them before we have a chance to second-guess him or deny His ability. I'd say it's high time we wake up and let the right people do the right things for once. Those who Accidentally Increase can be jerks at times just like you and me. Being a jerk apparently is not enough for God to disqualify you. All you jerks reading this already know it! Being a jerk is a part of being human. Part of *Accidental Increase* is realizing that you are *not* perfect and then coming to terms with it in a most glorious fashion.

Learning to accept normal idiocy (as opposed to abnormal idiocy — drooling and the like) will increase your effectiveness. Do yourself and the rest of the world a favor. Don't waste time believing it's not true! I have come to terms with this and it has been the biggest push forward for me. As I previously stated, it is far more productive to know what you are not than to know what you are. Knowing what you can't do means you don't have to waste time lying and pretending it's not true. You're going to find out anyway and then you'll have to waste even more time cleaning up the mess. I make

---

7 1Corinthians 1:26-31; Crazy talk!

it a point not to spend time with anyone who doesn't like me as much as I like them. That way my time with people is always profitable because they will equally invest in me as I do in them. Many people waste precious time with those who don't care anything about what they say — I don't.

"It's far more productive to know what you are not than to know what you are. Knowing what you can't do means you don't have to waste time lying and pretending it's not true."

I'll never forget the time a woman came up to me in church and asked me if I would visit her husband in the hospital. You might think I would have been eager to help, but after a couple of questions, I soon realized I was in deep Ju-Ju. After inquiring about her relationship with her husband, her answer surprised me. It was terrible. He was terrible to her and had been for many years. My second question went something like this; *"Does your husband want to see me…did he ask to see someone like me… someone who will speak as I speak?"* Her answer was "no" and so was mine. I made the spot decision to not spend my time with someone uninterested in listening, despite the unfortunate circumstance. She just looked at me like an aborigine staring at a ferris wheel[8] and I didn't apologize for it. I didn't have time. You have to qualify your time, and if you do, you will have more of it. This guy wasn't a good jerk by the way — he was a bad jerk! There is a difference and people who *"increase"* know it.

Broken Pots

I don't know about you, but my pot has a crack in it. I think this is why God created butts. He wants us to live in reminder that we are broken. Everybody is broken because if you try to plug the hole, you will kill a person (Ask Hitler's doctors about this.[9]) Broken is good. It's how it's supposed to be — for now.

---

8 I stole this from Dr. Phil.
9 It is widely speculated that improper treatment of Hitler's chronic intestinal ailments may have contributed to his poor health.

Understanding and agreeing with your brokenness creates great increase in your life. As I described in a very brief statement within the preface of the book, I had a rather hideous childhood when it came to my social network. This has contributed to my brokenness as a person among jerks — "good" jerks that is. The fact that I was a social misfit had long lasting effects on my life even up to the age of 39. But when I turned 40, an amazing thing happened. I was asked to work with the youth group at a church. At that time, many valuable people saw me as one who could bring some fresh ideas into an already thriving group of teens. Several people in leadership asked if I would share some of my story involving my 3 years as a professed agnostic. This was nearly 10 years after seminary, which is another book, I'm afraid.

I will say this much though, anybody claiming that God may not exist or that he is too distant to be involved, is angry and hurt on some molecular quantum level. There are three kinds of agnostics. Firstly, there are those who claim that the chances of knowing for certain whether or not there is a God cannot be known so they stop trying. Secondly, there are those who claim they don't know, but would love to find out. And lastly, there are those who simply don't care. Ignorance is bliss. That's the stupid one, in my opinion. I fit into the second category for reasons I don't have time to go into. However, I will say that just like Dorothy in the *Wizard of Oz*, I have since realized that what I was after was right in my own backyard the whole time.

Back to the youth group story, when I was first asked about sharing with the kids, I flatly declined. I told them that I couldn't stand teenagers and that they wouldn't care to listen to me. Fortunately they (and God) pursued me with relentless aggression and I finally gave in — maybe just to shut them up. What happened next was totally unexpected. After completing three, one-hour weekly discussions with these kids, I received a standing ovation. My eyes flooded with tears and I wasn't sure why. This occasion led me to embark on a quest that I didn't even know I was on. I ultimately ended up joining the group of teens, along with several other groups in New Hampshire, for a winter retreat.

I agreed to do a workshop because there weren't enough leaders to pull it off. When it was announced I would be one of the speakers, my group of about 23 teens erupted in applause, to my complete horror and fascination. Once again my eyes flooded up with what seemed like a dam of water ready to burst through my face! My class was standing room only (some had to sit on the floor) for both sessions. Upon arriving home, I began leading a small teen Bible study on Monday nights. One particular week, we were praying before we dismissed and suddenly it happened…the crazy talk!

A 13-year-old boy named Dennis[10] said he had something to tell me. It was a message from God and he was the kid scheduled to deliver it. Dennis was a boy that God obviously drafted. This kid was real green. He didn't know all the Christian lingo or the hallmark tone and false humility which many religious folks tend to mask themselves with. He was just himself. He looked down towards the floor and claimed that he had seen a toymaker in his mind's eye. The toymaker was picking up and examining the toys as they slowly moved by on a conveyer belt, making sure each one was in perfect working order. Dennis' eyes squinted with eager anticipation of his next image to deliver. He said that the toymaker was waiting for the special toys, those that needed special attention for no apparent reason.

When one of the special toys made its way past, he stopped the belt, picked it up the toy and worked on it extra special for several moments before restarting the belt. This only happened about once in every 400 toys. Dennis then looked me dead in the face and said, "You're one of those special toys." The dam broke right there in front of 14 kids. I wept like a baby. I didn't know what was wrong with me at 40 years of age. That is when I heard the voice of God myself. He told me that and for the first time in my life, a peer affirmed me. He said that I never emotionally matured beyond the age of 13 because I didn't have the tools. Dennis was 13. When I was 13, it was my worst year ever. That was the year I was kicked by a teacher, beat up by a girl, knocked unconscious by 11 kids, had my ears boxed in the school hallway and was locked in the gym locker in my underwear and left for dead!

For the first time in my entire life, a teenager told me I was special and I could not contain the emotions that followed. Before this day, even as a man I would always be intimidated by teens at the mall that looked me in the eye. I never shared this silent fear with anyone. But that Monday night when I got home it was gone. My heart had been healed by a 13-year-old boy who dared to speak the words of God to a 40-year-old man who didn't know why

---

10 Dennis Cronin is a freak of nature in my book... a hero to me.

he struggled with so much inferiority. I am not the same. I will never be the same. The largest crack in my 40-year-old pot was repaired. Later that week my mind was invaded with the image of a man's hand sewing up a human heart that had been torn wide open. I knew it was my heart and somehow I knew it was the hand of the Christ. I welcomed the surgery.

Stupid People with Bright Ideas

As one who has lucid moments of stupidity, I can also attest to the fact that I have had several bright ideas along the way. Part of the AI[11] (Accidental Increase) process, is knowing a bright idea when it shows up in front of you or ends up lodged within your cranial globe for some weird reason. Part of my process is consistently being on the lookout for these bright ideas in the first place. I have always been an opportunist in the sense that I know opportunity is always lurking in the shadows. It's up to me to be awake when it makes its way to the door. Those who live in the realm of AI know that you win some and you lose some and we're OK with this. Successful people never have a problem with scrutiny. They don't mind sharing their ideas and placing them within a forum for discussion and approval. They don't seem to mind when their idea is laughed at or scorned by people that matter, or tweaked by those who have a much stronger mind.

"Successful people never have a problem with scrutiny. They don't mind sharing their ideas and placing them within a forum for discussion and approval."

I have consistently made a habit of sharing my thoughts with people who are a whole lot smarter than me. Through this process, I have experienced far more success than failure. Years ago, I had a thriving custom painting business that allowed me to use my hands as well as my ingenuity. This was a terrific forum for bright ideas. For years, I went under the name of *S.M. Sisler Painting Co.* and that seemed to do just fine, but after a conversation

---

11 Not to be confused with Artificial Intelligence.

with my brother-in-law, I got a bright idea! Why not change the name of the company to something more interesting and appealing? What I came up with was *Dreamkote*. That name alone sparked a color change, a website, business cards, and let's not forget about the infamous 5-year Dreamkote Warrantee!

Here's the deal; Dreamkote was just a seed. That one bright idea made the company's final 5 years the most productive and fun years of its existence. When I changed the name, I had four contracts to paint already signed and awaiting my start. I came up with a 5-year warrantee including labor — which was unheard of. I called it the Dreamkote System. I charged an extra $2,000 and every person who was scheduled to paint wanted it! I made $8,000 that day after making just four phone calls, and so my Dreamkote journey began. Each new idea was birthed from the first one because it was pregnant with entrepreneurial life.

Dreamkote quickly became a household name within the area and its reputation spread rapidly. The Dreamkote font was the Aladdin Style and it was gold. It made you think of a magic carpet ride. I had more fun with the name than I did with the business itself! My focus shifted from painting to developing concepts and more ideas. It was as if that one bright idea caused an internal explosion within my synapses and all the entrepreneurial muck oozed from my cranial ball of mish-mash creating more and more ideas on its way down!

Elias Howe, the inventor of the sewing machine, once explained how the idea of a needle with a hole in the 'wrong end' came to him. Elias was in the middle of a dream where Indians were firing arrows through cloth, snagging threads and drawing the threads through with the tips of the arrows. Elias awoke and rushed to his workshop to put his "dream" into practice. The rest, as they say, is history. This was *his* bright idea. Having a bright idea is one thing — acting on it is another.

One of the biggest misunderstandings surrounding the bright idea concept is that only smart people have them. This is not true at all. Millions of stupid people have bright ideas each and every day. The problem is they lack the courage to act upon them. Those with AI take chances. They jump off cliffs and build their wings on the way down and many times forget the duct tape. Don't become the person who at the end of their life sits down with their great grandchildren and tells stories about what they could have done. I don't mind if you are stupid, but don't add insult to injury by refusing to act upon your bright ideas. I am writing this book because it's a bright idea.

Every human being has lucid moments of stupidity. Every one. Never forget that. Some people are just experts at making you believe it isn't so. We are all in the same pool folks — the sea of humanity. As a behavioral consultant, I interact with CEO's from all over the east coast and frankly many of them are missing a few fries out of the Happy Meal®. Some of them have only two things going for them; money and risk — that's it. They are completely devoid of brain matter. If it weren't for several key individuals, they would be sucking pond water from a nasty straw. Once I gain an audience with some of these people, their blind spots become apparent almost immediately. They are just like you and me.

Their success comes from a combination of guts, fortitude, risk, determination, etc. — notice I didn't say brains! This is because what they all have in common is an inability to get it all completely right. Many times they overdose on stupid pills before coming to work and that's usually when I end up in their office. What you need to understand is this — we all have our assets and liabilities. No one has *only* assets. You have just as much a chance to do something spectacular as the next person. You simply have to be willing to take that chance, and put your butt on the line. Will it pan out? Maybe it will or maybe it won't. So what, eventually one of your ideas will. Every person who has experienced any kind of success has capitalized on the one idea that worked.

So the next time you have a bright idea, share it with those who matter in your life, those who love and appreciate you in spite of your stupidity. If they all believe it's ridiculous then you are forced to determine whether or not it's going to be a smart move or a heart move. Either way, it's your move so be proud of it.

7

The "I" Triangle

The Power of Insecurity

"Stop acting as if life is a rehearsal. Live this day as if it were your last. The past is over and gone. The future is not guaranteed."

— WAYNE DYER

The Fear of Not Being Liked

All High Influence[1] people have a fear of not being liked. 23 years ago, early on in my marriage, I ran with all my might into a block wall of cement. My wife and I were living in Broken Arrow, OK and I was starting my first year of seminary. While I was working hard at my studies, my wife was working lots of hours at a car dealership. A few of the salesmen there took an interest in my beautiful bride and one of them even asked her to lunch. Of course, she flatly turned him down. Upon telling me this story however, I became *stricken* with jealousy and fear. With my insecurity running overtime, I began dropping stupid little comments in an attempt to thwart the situa-

---

1 The "I" in the DISC Analysis assessment — represents a very magnetic, emotional and chatty style of behaving.

tion, but in the process unwittingly entered my first year of *Moron School*.[2] I began saying things like; "You probably like him better than me anyway..." or "He has a lot more money than I do...you'd be better off with him." and other bird-brained statements of choice. I suppose this was my backwards attempt to make her feel sorry for me. It didn't work. As a matter of fact, it backfired.

What exactly happened next is between me and my dog Duke. I will never be able to fully explain it and neither Duke nor I will ever be quite the same.[3] That said, to this day I am forever grateful for it. There I was lying in bed at home extremely ill, but sound asleep. As normal, my wife went off early to work. Lying there, I abruptly heard the sound of my name shouted into my ear. It apparently was so loud that Duke also woke up and ran through the apartment barking like a mad lunatic. "OK. Who is at the door, Duke?" I said. The dog paced and barked through the family room and hall as if someone was in the house, but I couldn't see who or what Duke was all worked up about. I chalked it up as *zoo phenomenon*[4] and went back to bed. Almost instantaneously I heard within my mind the words "Proverbs 11:11" over and over again. It was so strong that I retrieved a Bible and read the passage.

This is what it said; "*Through the blessing of the upright a city is exalted, but by the mouth of the wicked it is destroyed.*"[5] I suddenly realized who had been in my room. God was speaking at that very moment and I surmised that this is what he meant. I was destroying my wife (the city) by my wicked mouth and stupid comments. I started to weep uncontrollably. When my wife came home later that evening, I shared this extraordinary tale with her and she told me something equally amazing. She had been praying the very night before that God would speak to me about my weird behavior because she did not know how much longer she could stand it! I repented of my actions and asked her to forgive me, which she gladly did. God loves to answer prayer when he's the only option you have left. Thanks to my wife's prayer, I bounced off the block wall and somehow survived!

---

2 The School of Hard Knox for people with a habit of being an idiot (a lifelong education for some). I graduated Magna Cum Laude in 2003.
3 Especially Duke because he's dead now.
4 When all the best animals at the zoo mysteriously vanish after you have paid to see them.
5 Proverbs 11:11: Obviously one of my all time favorites. This verse probably saved my marriage in 1986.

I am using this personal illustration to show you that there is a good healthy fear, and then there is the fear called paranoia, which will destroy you. The fear of not being liked can be a great asset as long as you know how to attach healthy boundaries to it. If you don't know you have it, it might end up having you, as referenced in my last story.

OK, we're going to have to run a bit deeper now to understand the "whys" and "how's" of behavior. If you can stay with me on this, it might help you understand why you behave the way you do. Once you understand that, then we can work on some strategies to help you avoid hitting the block wall.

For all you black and white thinkers (I am one, as well), try to hang in there, because as people we are all actually "crafted" by God in very unique and wonderful ways. There are overreaching rules that apply to behavior, but there are also subtle differences within each person. Think snowflake. A snowflake is a snowflake, yet there is not one that is exactly alike another. So in people, there are four primary emotions and these emotions act as the basis of behavior. It's the combination of all four in varying strengths that lead to a particular style of how one will conduct themselves. Like the primary[6] colors, the mixing of any other emotions within your soul does not create these four basic emotions. So for example, mixing two colors together cannot create the color red. You also cannot create the primary colors yellow or blue. But by mixing these three colors, you can create over 16 million colors! It's a veritable nuclear reaction that just keeps on going. I want to list for you now the four basic human emotions that when mixed, create the way you act out your intentions from within. They are; anger, optimism, fear and the ability to mask your emotions. Some may call it mad, glad, sad and scared. The fact is your emotional makeup basically revolves around the energy of these four.

The High Influence person usually has three fears and they are as follows... not being liked, failure, and being misunderstood. This creates a very powerful dynamic because it deals with highly emotional behavior. If you are a High Influence person, your struggle will be to learn to be consistent when everything and everyone is falling down around you. You also tend to think

---

6 Red, Yellow and Blue - you cannot create these colors using any other color within the colors we know of; I find this very weird believe it or not, but if you mix blue & yellow you create green and so on.

with your mouth rather than your brain. You wear your heart on your sleeve and because you are such an open book, most people will really like who you are. By the same token, your driving desire to be liked means you will tend to make emotional appeals in order to get your way with others. Put simply, you like to persuade people. You will be more enthusiastic, more creative and more persuasive than others who are logic based in their emotional makeup. Many people assume that the opposite of optimism is pessimism, but I beg to differ. The opposite of optimism is logic based reasoning void of emotional appeal. The one who needs to be liked will try to shape their environment through persuasive techniques while those who are more logical will stick to a matter-of-fact set of tools. Logic based people think this way, "*If you don't like me, that's your problem.*"

The fear of not being liked comes from a very "*need based*" emotion. All High Influence people will find that their requirement based on needing to be liked is an option that is more viable and attractive than the need to be correct. There are also those who operate this way, but have come to know themselves so well that they no longer need to be liked - they like being liked. I would suggest that there's a big difference here and it in fact makes all the difference in the world.

The need to be liked will cause you to manipulate any situation involving other people into a positive experience so that everyone involved comes away liking you as well as the interactive moments with you. This is the power of insecurity at work. To be honest, about 10 years ago, I was the most insecure person you would ever meet.[7] Being insecure most of my life has been the catapult that has thrown me forward where I otherwise would not have attempted to go. It quite frankly boils down to a security in who we are.

It's funny how being insecure can actually work to your advantage as long as you aren't obnoxious about it. Unfortunately, some folks are far too over the top with their need-based issues. You should be aware that you have a tendency towards constant jibber-jabber and *emotional appeals*. Realize that you can be a drama queen at the drop of a hat. This lack of emotional intelligence causes your emotions to work against you when interacting with

---

7 I started figuring this out in 1999.

others who are more secure. The ability to manage your emotions comes in handy for the High Influencer.

Accidental Increase happens when a High Influence person knows their need-based weakness and is able to wield it like a sword for the benefit of all involved. For instance, knowing when to be quiet and when to come on strong (verbally) will increase your communication ability dramatically. Not knowing these things can be social suicide in most situations.

Many people have crashed and burned simply because they didn't know when to shut up! Nervous laughter, loud and constant talking and consistently bringing the topic back to you are true killers. This takes place when you are both insecure and have low EQ (Emotional Quotient) — bummer of a situation here. If this is you, it's time to get a handle on yourself. It's amazing what people will do when they are overly self-centered and consumed with what others think of them.

Being excessively concerned with what others think about you is bad Ju-Ju.[8] Accidental Increase takes place when you really don't care what others think. This is not an excuse for psychotic behavior. Brushing your teeth and combing your hair is always a good idea! What I'm trying to say is that you must learn to be comfortable with yourself "as is." Those who increase have bought into themselves "as is" and they don't apologize for it. This is a great place to be. You don't have to become an actor or actress when dealing with other people at home or at the office—you're just comfortable in your own skin, comfortable with who God made you to be. Consistently trying to win the approval of others can get mighty tiresome.

If you can't get up in the morning and look at yourself naked in the mirror and at least consider it a good joke, then you are not in the best place. If this kind of thing produces depression or anxiety then you may need to fall in love with yourself all over again. Self-acceptance paves the way to acceptance of oth-

"If you can't get up in the morning and look at yourself naked in the mirror and at least consider it a good joke, then you are not in the best place."

---

8 Ju-Ju is like a bad omen. Bad Ju-Ju is like a *really* bad omen.

ers. If you can't accept yourself, you will end up trying far too hard to sell yourself to everyone else. You're not supposed to be *for sale* anyway!

Fear of Failure

Fear of failure can be debilitating, but it can also be an opportunity to increase by accident. Those with a high emotional level and an optimistic viewpoint will want to win in life, not because they love winning, but because they hate losing. Wanting to win because you love winning creates energy, but wanting to win because you hate losing creates an aura. Call it the power of negative thinking, but if you're floating out at sea and you desperately do not want to drown, you will last much longer than the one who just wants to live.[9]

It's this fear of failure that creates the incredible energy necessary for large entrepreneurial ideas and big dreams. Those who don't fear failure will always run the risk of being overly confident and doing the jerk dance.[10] If the fear of failure is completely non-existent, incisiveness will set in with a matter-of-fact non-emotional based style that will ultimately turn people off. This is when you become *completely* task-oriented and begin to view people as merely objects of use or obstacles to avoid. This usually is caused by not caring what others think times ten. You become virtually silent, moody and robotic in nature - an android of sorts. Everyone's afraid at times, but being fearful is a *real* problem. Similarly, I like being alone, but being lonely would be bad Ju-Ju for sure.

Failure is Not an Option

Failure is not an option. That's how I think most of the time and it's turned out to be an asset. It always brings me back to the "no plan B" model. It has motivated me to take some good healthy risks. Those who fear failure will tend to risk certain things. They will bargain or gamble circumstances in order to ensure that they don't fail. It may sound like a paradox, but they

---

9 I made this observation in 2008 during a behavioral debrief.
10 The jerk dance is when you think way too much of yourself and end up emotionally dancing your way out of a stupid situation with everyone looking on in disbelief.

THE "I" TRIANGLE   93

actually take more chances than those who don't fear failure. These people will become extremely creative in order to ensure success. They don't give talks; they are the grand finales because they cannot fail. They will stay up all night and memorize the whole presentation if need be. You can see how fearing failure can become a weapon of influence when the right magical balance is struck.

Accidental Increase comes when a high EQ level joins the fear of failure and together they wow the crowd for just the right amount of time. They leave the audience wanting more. Haven't we seen Hollywood take advantage of this with their investment in great sequels and prequels? What is *Star Wars* without the *Empire Strikes Back* and *Return of the Jedi*? This is the height of playing to your strengths and your weaknesses. The goal is to be able to *capitalize* on your strengths and *embrace* your weaknesses because they work together. You cannot have one without the other and they are both *equally* important! Many people try to capitalize on their strengths while at the same time hating their weaknesses, treating them like the enemy or the emotional plague. This will not work for you. But don't worry my young Padawan apprentice; we'll cover more of this in chapter 9.

Fear of Being Misunderstood

Accidental Increase takes place when you fear being misunderstood. This will cause you to cover all the bases in an attempt to be clear, concise and thorough. Again, it takes strong EQ to pull this off nicely; otherwise you're just talking too much. You have to be careful about how much information you give people. High EQ enables you to read the body language of the listener, watching for signs of frustration and boredom. When someone consistently looks at his or her watch, it may be time to call it a day. Solomon says that a sensible person (*discreetly*) hides knowledge, but foolish minds preach stupidity.[11]

There is always a balance to these things and being the one who strikes it right makes all the difference in the world. It could be the difference between getting or not getting a new job. Making yourself clear with your words

---

11 My paraphrase of Proverbs 12:23

> "When you combine the fear of not being liked with the fear of failure and then pile on the fear of being misunderstood, you have the making of an incredibly powerful persuasion tool provided they are all balanced correctly."

is an art. Speaking lots of nonsense is a mess.[12] Having a heightened awareness of such things is a definite asset. Do not be clueless here or it could prove deadly in the wrong situation. When you combine the fear of not being liked with the fear of failure and then pile on the fear of being misunderstood, you have the making of an incredibly powerful persuasion tool provided they are all balanced correctly. If any one of these fears is out of whack, social disaster could ensue. Just don't give up! Stay in the place of knowing that God really appreciates you, despite the screw-ups.

As long as these emotions are coupled with the healthy concern for others and a healthy view of self as we mentioned earlier, beautiful things will happen and yes, by accident. This way of life will create very successful relationships over the long haul.

The Eros Prison

The lack of ability to socially produce positive results in others is what creates the "Eros prison." Eros in its root form means "the sum of all instincts for self-preservation."[13] Although there are variations and degrees of self-centeredness, the results always remain constant. The Eros prison is a state of continued self-centeredness. This is usually common among people with addictions that are not only harmful to themselves, but to all of their interpersonal relationships as well. In an effort to "protect" those around them, addicts will keep all the important people in the dark while they fall prey to their own self-absorbed behaviors — yikes!

---

12 Another one of my off the cuff proverbs.
13 The term Eros, as defined by dictionary.com (Self-preservation begins with Eros while love begins with Agape)

These behaviors may include drug addictions, sexual addictions and the like, accompanied by sulking, mood swings, self-hatred, and an inability to live up to high personal standards. Regardless of the kind of behavior, the inability to openly share with anyone is equally detrimental. What you are experiencing in these situations tends to tightly bind the behavior and its results around you, thus producing a straitjacket effect. This is when you become your own worst enemy. Like a bacterium, you will tend to isolate yourself from others and bury yourself in an emotional closet. The problem with all this is something I call the Godzilla Conundrum. While hidden away in the closet, your addiction runs the risk of turning into Godzilla and without warning will turn around and eat you.

Let me explain what Godzilla looks like from a very personal perspective. Once upon a time many years ago, my wife was headed out to a women's retreat. She had placed the kids with a sitter until I was finished with my responsibilities at work and so I decided it was a brilliant idea[14] to rent and watch a mature video before picking them up. I went to "Video for All" and remember picking it out and hiding it until all was clear (so far-so good). The moment I came up with this devious plot was the moment I entered what I call the bubble.[15]

The most important thing to know about the bubble is this; you have to leave your brain with all its logical reasoning *outside*. There I was at 31 years of age, sitting in my underwear on the living room floor, watching my precious video. My wife, who had forgot hotdogs for the trip, came bursting through the door and walked right into my worst, most awful place! It was one of the most embarrassing and humiliating moments of my life. Godzilla had eaten through everything I called sane and pure and I hadn't even realized it. What was left was a broken relationship and spirit and it was entirely *my* fault. I had been feeding this pig for months.

I can remember riding down the road in tears screaming out the window towards an

> "While hidden away in the closet, your addiction runs the risk of turning into Godzilla and without warning will turn around and eat you."

14 Welcome to the satanic mind meld. When in the "Mind Meld," stupid appears to be brilliant!
15 When in the "Bubble," all brain matter is lost. Your stupidity at once agrees with you.

open feild, "*I'm a pornographer!*" I had to face the reality of the situation if I was going to get out of it. God had to reveal the Godzilla in my life to bring me to the place where he could begin the process of healing me at his cross. I love my wife and I love my children. I would never do anything to betray that trust. This is how I feel, but there have been points where Godzilla runs amuck and rampages out of control eating everything you know to be sane! Do you know that it takes *courage* to face reality?[16] This is because courage is truly the *absence of self* whereas cowardice is the fullness of self.

When we constantly live a life of self-focus and convoluted intension because we are overly concerned about not being liked or fearing failure, we negate the power and freedom available to us through selflessness. Jesus is our model for such behavior. His focus was always outward. He was the opposite of an emotionally disadvantaged person. He was a life *giving* spirit.[17] If we are to succeed socially, we must first jump the hurdle of self-addiction and self-pity and embrace others. We must allow ourselves to be expensed during the process of human interaction. The ability to get along without constant emotional stimulation brings health and well being not only to you, but also to those around you.

The Wisdom of the Skin Horse

Those who increase accidentally are always real. They also tend to be relevant, responsible and reliable. In her classic children's book "*The Velveteen Rabbit*,"[18] Margery Williams writes profoundly about being real. In this remarkable story, we follow the journey of a small stuffed toy rabbit in his search for identity and self worth. The rabbit encounters the old skin horse, a sort of patriarchal figure with EQ on steroids. The skin horse has lived his best years in a little boy's nursery observing the personal identity struggles of all the other toys. When the little rabbit struggles to find purpose, he asks the skin horse if he understands what the term real actually means.

---

16 Coined by the late Dr. Edwin Louis Cole (born Dallas, Texas in 1922, died August 27, 2002) in 1989.
17 1 Corinthians 15:45: The Spiritual did not come first; the natural did. See vs. 46-47's earth/heaven analogy.
18 Published in 1922 by Double Day and Company, Inc. Garden City, New York.

This is a very profound question seeing that most people find their worth in what they do as opposed to who they actually are.[19]   In the case of the Velveteen Rabbit, we find the same dynamic at work within a small group of nursery toys and discover how the wisdom of the skin horse helps guide the little rabbit into a place of self-acceptance. Ultimately, this leads to him becoming a real rabbit — which is where we all want to be — real that is, not necessarily a rabbit.

"What is REAL?" asked the Rabbit one day, when they were lying side by side near the nursery fender, before Nana came to tidy the room.

"Does it mean having things that buzz inside you and a stick-out handle?"

"Real isn't how you are made," said the Skin Horse. "It's a thing that happens to you. When a child loves you for a long, long time, not just to play with, but REALLY loves you, then you become Real."

"Does it hurt?" asked the Rabbit.

"Sometimes," said the Skin Horse, for he was always truthful. "When you are Real you don't mind being hurt."

"Does it happen all at once, like being wound up," he asked, "or bit by bit?"

"It doesn't happen all at once," said the Skin Horse. "You become. It takes a long time. That's why it doesn't happen often to people who break easily, or have sharp edges, or who have to be carefully kept. Generally, by the time you are Real, most of your hair has been loved off, and your eyes drop out and you get loose in the joints and very shabby. But these things don't matter at all, because once you are Real you can't be ugly, except to people who don't understand."

"I suppose you are real?" said the Rabbit. And then he wished he had not said it, for he thought the Skin Horse might be sensitive. But the Skin Horse only smiled.

In his wisdom, the skin horse breaks the relationship issue down to its simplest form. Like a reduced fraction, he subtracts all the unnecessary elements from the equation and presents the Velveteen Rabbit with his answer.

"Being real is when you are loved for who you are." When we project pretend images to those around us, we end up with pretend relation-

---
19 Human-doings as opposed to human-beings.

ships, pretend friendships and pretend marriages. Love becomes a movie or a fairytale reserved for bedside reading. We spend the rest of our life trying to hold on to the make believe relationships through a process of continued scheming and relentless pretending. We need to enter a place of true friendship where vital aspects of life are talked about and worked on.

Friendship is a relationship that is entirely based on trust.
Friendship is respect.
Friendship is loyalty.
Friendship is association.
Friendship involves the exchange of ideas, thoughts, knowledge and cultural
values.
Friendship is solidarity.
Friendship is not subjection.

The basis of friendship is actually covenantal in that it is expressed in the very core of who God is and the type of relationship that he desires. The term, "a friend who sticks closer than a brother"[20] implies covenant. A covenantal relationship was meant to be stronger than even family relations. We get glimpses of what true friendship looks like in the Bible with a bird's eye view of David and Jonathan. We also see it in the relationship between Abraham and God.[21]

The ancient Hebrew ritual of becoming friends was comprised of a nine step process involving blood and vows. Hence the biblical references; *"I no longer call you servants, ...but friends"*[22] and *"...he (Abraham) was called God's friend."*[23] A friend knows your business...all of it! Therefore I do not intrude upon the lifestyles of acquaintances. If an individual does not understand and appreciate where you are, where you want to be, or where you have been, then you are not in relationship with that person.

Real friendships have a "no-risk" element to them while surface relationships can be very risky. Ultimately, we affect those around us more by

---

20 Proverbs 18:24
21 Genesis 15
22 John 15:15
23 James 2:23

accident than on purpose, true friends included. There are times of calling a friend to a higher standard of living, but now we are talking about the deepest level of friendship. This is when you are so completely aware of your love for one another that it qualifies you to say just about anything.

Relationships are primary, not instrumental. This is an important concept to remember. In the story of the Velveteen Rabbit, the jointed lion and the model boat are need oriented in their approach to relationship building. Their constant convoluted style keeps them forever focused on *self* at the *expense* of everyone else. The toy boat boasts of his exterior rigging apparatus' in an attempt to belittle the rabbit's rather plain exterior. Meanwhile, the jointed wooden lion boasts about his being made by the local disabled soldiers and therefore claims connections to the government.[24] This is the process of association and unfortunately typical.

The lion has found an opportunity to associate with what he perceives to be a respectable party and then attempts to align himself with the character of his new found associates. When people have no character of their own, they identify with those whom they believe to have acceptable character. Through this process of identification they will name-drop and reference the party and ultimately take on the character of the identified party through what is known as personification.

Like these mechanical toys, we too might be tempted to delve into modernistic notions of being in an attempt to shed the shell of what we believe to be a boring human condition. This is a most unwise and destructible path to tread. When we focus on the outside, we miss the most important place of all - the inside. The young rabbit and the skin horse ultimately end up in a much different and deeper reality. The rabbit, because of his openness and ability to accept himself for who he *really* is, transforms from an object to a life giving spirit.

The Death That Counts

In 2001 I died the death that counts. In order to die the death that counts, you must be content to *"know* nothing," *"do* nothing," and be *"known for*

---

24 I knew an insecure woman who once pointed to a passenger in an old painting of the Mayflower claiming, "Oh, there we are!" She desperately wanted an important heritage.

nothing." If you cannot do this, you will live a life of struggling with your personal identity.

The death that counts takes place when you are no longer trying to protect yourself and your reputation from harm. You don't "need" to be in charge. You don't "need" people to know what you do for a living. You don't "need" people to know how important your position is, etc. You just are. You are fully content with your position in life, your mate, your children, your height, your weight, your car, etc. This doesn't mean that you won't try to lose weight if it get's out of a healthy range; it means that you are just trying to be more health conscious.

Many people are NOT content with who they are anstruggle with having to prop up exterior things like their job or looks in order to make up for the discontentedness within. Selfish ambition and controlling issues all find their roots in this insecure place. The day you find complete contentment in knowing nothing; not having to spit out everything you think you know on a subject when in a crowd of people. Doing nothing; having to show great feats of accomplishment for fear of looking lazy. Being known for nothing; not having to slip your great accomplishments into every situation for fear of not looking smart or successful, will be the greatest and most liberating day of your life.

8

Accidental Increase

The Power of Chance

"Now that I look back, I realize that a life predicated on being obedient and taking orders is a very comfortable life indeed. Living in such a way reduces to a minimum one's need to think."

— ADOLF EICHMANN

I Never Wanted this Job in the First Place

People of Accidental Increase more often than not are on a mission. They are passing through this world with a job to do and somehow, through words and deeds, they get it done. These missions take place at work, home and other unique places. I remember very clearly a day in 1989. I was painting the side of a building with some co-workers. Without warning, something came over me like a wind. I leaned over to the guy next to me and said, *"If you don't do something about your drug addiction and your dysfunctional life, you will end up in prison!"* I was mortified by these words escaping my lips but I could not contain them. Sure enough, the person I spoke this warning to ended up in prison sometime later — I connected with him on FaceBook recently. Now, I didn't want that to happen and I don't think God did either! Another bizarre story is found in the Old Testament in the book of Amos. Amos is considered to be a minor prophet by scholars, Jews and Christians alike. Have you ever heard the name Amos? He is certainly not as well known as Jeremiah or Daniel. At this time in history, Israel was split into two kingdoms: Israel and Judah. Without getting into too much detail, Amos prophesied against both Israel and Judah as well as to the Gentile nations.

Amos was "...*among the herdsmen of Tekoa*." This is a nice way of saying that he was a goat herder. What I appreciate about this story is that Amos was drafted into one of the worst jobs imaginable. Still, he found a way to get it accomplished. As this story proceeds, enter Amaziah. He was a priest paid by the king to proclaim blessings for the king and for Israel. This was an alliance between religion and the autocracy — a recipe for disaster! What Amaziah didn't do was to tell the king the truth. Meanwhile, old Amos was telling the truth. To his detriment, he was prophesying against King Jeroboam and all of Israel. I suppose it is a bummer to have to preach against an Old Testament king in his own land. Amos was akin to The Far Side comic strip with the deer that has a large "X" inscribed over his chest.

Not surprisingly, we read that Amaziah (the king's butt boy) sent the following message to Jeroboam. "*Amos is raising a conspiracy against you in the very heart of Israel. The land cannot bear all his words, for this is what Amos is saying: Jeroboam will die by the sword, and Israel will surely go into exile, away from their native land*."

He also writes Amos as well by saying, "*Get out of here you seer! Go back to your own land and earn your bread and tell your stories there! You're just making trouble for everyone here*."[1] Amaziah's life boiled down to proclaiming good omens for money and he simply assumed that Amos would catch a bad case of "leavingitus" based on finances or lack of them. He obviously didn't know anything about Amos' CQ[2] levels.

Amos retorted, "I was neither a prophet, nor a prophets son, but I was a shepherd and a keeper of sycamore-fig trees... you knucklehead!" (OK, I added "you knucklehead!"). In other words, Amos is saying that he never

1 Paraphrased from Amos 7:10-17
2 Character Quotient (See chapter 1)

wanted this job in the first place! He may have been a simple shepherd, but he had more courage in his little finger than all of Israel.

One day in 1998, while painting a barn in Massachusetts, once again something came over me. This time it was a terrible foreboding that caused me to tremble. I was getting words in my head that were so powerful I got down off the ladder and wrote them on a napkin that I found on the floorboard of my truck. It was a message directed to my sister's husband. The message was quite bold. In fact, it was outright audacious. I didn't quite know what to do with it. For the sake of my sister's privacy, I won't go into specific details. The basic message was this: "*If you do not deal with this issue, you will first lose your mind, then your family and then your own life.*" Whaaat?!! This was the first time such a thought had ever crossed my mind. To be honest, I wasn't even aware that my sister's husband struggled with this particular issue.

The feeling was so strong that I made my way back to my office and immediately placed a call to him. It was the middle of the day, but I didn't care. Surprisingly, he answered the phone. I pulled out the napkin and read him the words that I had inscribed. Then I gritted my teeth and waited in silence. The tension was quite palpable. "This is lunacy," I thought. Then, to my utter shock, he broke down right there on the phone and admitted it was all true! He had been fighting with this issue and so we talked about it for over three hours. I offered him hope and encouragement, and did the best I could to help him heed the warning. We had such a wonderful, heartfelt conversation that I thought surely he understood that the bridge ahead of his car was truly "out." Some time passed and he got back into his old habit. Eventually he did lose his mind and in a rage threatened to kill my parents and my brother! He also sent me a letter claiming I had tricked him by appealing to his emotions using "slight of hand" magic. From my standpoint, I knew that God had simply given me a job to do and I wasn't going to let him down. In return, my sister's husband threatened me, kicked my sister out and not long after, ended his own life. I am still grieved.

The Fat Lady

In 1997, while living in Florida, I received a call one day from a woman down the street. She and her husband rented a home within walking distance. I knew her because she had been at a few functions I attended, but to be honest I didn't really like her. As I remember, she was extremely overweight and needed the use of a walker to get around. She came across as prideful and headstrong, in my opinion. I therefore avoided her whenever I saw her in town. She called to inform me that she had given my name to her landlord and he would be calling me so that I could put in a bid for painting.

I wasn't very busy at the time so I welcomed the project although I did not like the idea of having to interact with her more than necessary. Unfortunately (so I thought) I got the call from the landlord and ended up scheduling the project. When I began the project, I remember standing on the ladder about a story high, painting the window sash over the front of this woman's rented home. I could see directly into the family room and noticed her sitting in a chair looking blankly at the wall without any emotion or movement. That's when it hit me. You know, that scary, freaky force from heaven… the mission. The reason I breathe!

My dirty, selfish, ignorant soul was flooded with a compassion I had never experienced before, or possibly since. My disdain and contempt for this poor woman flew from me like a bird.

This is what I heard in my head: *"You need to go down there and knock on the door and tell her that if she prays with you, I will heal her of her weight problem today."*

"I must be insane," I thought. *"What in the H-E-double hockey sticks is wrong with me?"* The feeling was so strong however, that I reluctantly put my tools away and went to the door. Despite being very weak in the knees, I managed to stand there for some time rehearsing the words in my mind. I found my hands trembling as I finally knocked on the door. Before I knew it, there she was asking me what I wanted. Now how on God's green earth was I going to answer that question? I asked her if I could come in to speak with her for just a minute. She agreed and let me in the home. I sat across from her and without much more thought, launched myself off the precipice to whatever ends.

"I got the crazy feeling that I needed to pray for you. If you allow me to, I believe that God will help you with your weight problem. I hope this isn't offend-

ing you, but I didn't know what else to do." She looked at me and started to weep uncontrollably.

"My father died yesterday and he went to the grave absolutely hating me because I am fat," she said.

"It's as if I'm a leper. I can't even go to the store without people stopping to stare at me."

It reminded me of how Jesus must have felt looking at the crowds with nothing to offer but a petition to the Father's heart. How do we touch lepers? Love... true love. My eyes flooded over and I began to weep. I prayed for her through intermittent sobs along with a few words of encouragement. Her husband came home and joined us. What a moment that is frozen in the corners of my mind. God had helped a broken man like me to be used for his glory. He helped me to build my wings on the way down!

She and her husband visited me a few months later. She had lost 40 pounds since we last spoke! According to her, she had never done that before. Is this what I signed up for when I started the painting company or when I gave my life to God? No, but that's what I got. These things continue to this day and I could fill these pages with very similar stories, but here's the point — People of Accidental Increase allow the mission of heaven to flow through them each and every day. They are selfless and open to help all those around them. They, like Amos, open their mouths for the betterment of humanity without being cocky or prideful. Are you fighting your voice and chalking it up to silly nonsense? I have found that some of the most ridiculous, out-of-the-box notions have had the most profound impact on people.

Jump First, Decide Second

People of increase lead unpredictable lives much of the time. This is what I call the rhino approach to life. Living this way leaves about 12 inches of space for quick turns. People who learn to get comfortable with the uncomfortable learn to build their wings on the way down. It is all about leaving the safety of predictability and embarking on a pioneering adventure. So, get out your napkins and get ready for the windblown look with the salt spray in your face!

"Think about the rhino. The rhino can run 30 miles per hour but can only see 31 feet."

As you may have guessed, "building your wings on the way down" is one of my favorite sayings of all time.[3] The truth it holds is remarkable. It means that you don't have to be completely prepared in this life before acting on your reliable God given impulses, as long as you have learned to trust them. Think about the rhino. The rhino can run 30 miles per hour but can only see 31 feet ahead. If he makes a bad decision, he simply makes another decision to compensate. Likewise, through trial and error, we learn to run on instinct and faith rather than a plotted course. I would suggest that the margin for mistakes and victories is infinitesimal.

Chicks and Ducks, Conflict and Adversity

There are two things that we are all generally trying to avoid: conflict and adversity. I tend to like them both. Recently, I gave this fellow[4] at a conference some winning advice to leave his church over a particular issue he was having (*After a short discussion, it was apparent his family was being extremely over worked and under appreciated-in a bad way*). Later the district overseer informed me of his dissatisfaction for my opinion after finding out what I had said. I simply bowed low and deferred to the pastor's judgment, lest we both go careening off a cliff.

You've heard of the tale of the unborn chick haven't you? Allowing the chick to break from its shell independently is a must in nature. The effort required for shell deconstruction is the very thing the baby bird needs to build its strength for life on the outside. If you try to assist the chick in this endeavor by breaking its shell, you will only succeed in shortening its life span to hours or even minutes. Just like the young chick, we also need adversity to make our character strong. It all comes down to the usual suspects — conflict and adversity. There are so many times that I find myself face-flat on the ground. Yet, it is there, that God lifts my head to encourage me to

---

3 I cannot even remember where I saw this anymore — it hung on my fridge for a long time in early 2003.
4 This guy and his wife were youth pastors. They would have been better off working at Auschwitz.

keep going. Part of the key to this life is simply understanding that there is a God and that you are not him. Grabbing hold of this concept will allow you the freedom to take risks regardless of their initial success or failure. My friend once got this great word. "You are swimming in the deep end. There is no touching the bottom, but God is with you there." Having to have each and every duck in a row will prove fatal when it comes to increasing exponentially because unfortunately, ducks don't always come in rows.

Impatience is a Virtue

I am a very, very impatient person. In fact, I have the patience of a burnt tick. This is good. I used to not like it, but I have found over the years that it has dramatically increased my potential to increase. The secret is knowing when to be impatient. Being impatient at the burger stand and making everyone with you miserable is just being stupid. You have to learn to enjoy yourself and calm down. When impatience robs you of your joy, you have got bigger ticks in the backyard.

Impatience is always the product of *flexibility*.[5] Being able to turn on a dime is paramount in achieving successes faster. There is no need to wait on anything else. I will drive through to get the desired results and will hate waiting for everyone else to catch up. Of course, this also has its drawbacks. I moved my beloved family 1500 miles by accident once. That was a real bummer, but I made the best of it and also made many great memories and new friends that still play a very large role in our lives. Being a High Influence person helped me see things optimistically and therefore we forged ahead with much excitement and joy. It's important to find the good in your accidents... my daughter learned to walk in that house that was 1500 miles away.

Impatient people are the "people-movers." They are the drivers behind many inventions and new perspectives. Please don't misunderstand this position- we are not talking about the bad jerk here, but rather the one who takes the chance and delivers the goods because they were quick to act. This quickness is far more productive than the slow mover. Slow movers need to know what is around the corner all the time, but the impatient people actu-

---

5 Again, this may sound like a paradox but I've seen it at work firsthand.

ally like the surprise. I'm the type that if you viewed life as a forest, I would be the person running headlong blindfolded into the woods at full steam. Yes…if you're thinking that I'd also be the one to hit the first tree with a bloody thud, you'd be right on the money! It "smarts" for weeks after, believe me I know.

One time, I was painting a house and set the feet of my ladder in some sand; a construction no-no. It was the quickest way to "rhino" the job to completion. When I ascended with my paint bucket to get to the window trim a couple of stories up, wouldn't you know that the ladder started to slide? Like a cat, I dug my fingernails into the wooden shingles on the way to the ground. My friend saw the "claw marks" the next day. I ripped all the tendons off my foot, which now hurts every time the weather changes. Yet, I survived! Let's talk about that for a second. What's to say that every moment of your life actually isn't borrowed time? I love that song by Tim McGraw[6]: "I went sky diving. I went rocky mountain climbing. I went two point seven seconds on a bull named Fumanchu. And I loved deeper and I spoke sweeter. And I gave forgiveness I'd been denying. And he said one day I hope you get a chance to live like you were dying."

"To live is Christ, and to die is gain."[7] We are aliens folks. We are heading to a much better place, but here on earth we might as well live like we were dying. Those who live predictably are like a blind man. They find their way through the woods at an extremely slow pace, feeling with their hands extended. I will be out of the woods much faster, albeit minus an eye or even a limb. I will have started and failed three businesses by the time those who run the race with caution finish drawing up the plan for their first endeavor. I will follow this proven pathway to success…start-stop, start-stop, start-stop, start-fail, start-fail, start-fail, and then make it big!

Displaying Your Independence

I am an independent soul. I love to display the fact that I don't want to rely upon another for my successes or failures. Independent souls are the developers. We are after the unique accomplishments only. Anything less feels

---

6 Written by Tim Nichols and Craig Wiseman.
7 Philippians 1:21

like a straitjacket soaked in cold water. We want to be a part of the new opportunities, which includes being free of constraining group influences. Independent, self-willed and stubborn is our name. Out of the box we go!

This is why we tend to lead and rarely follow. Accidental Increase becomes a way of life for us. We fall in the sewer and rise smelling like a rose.[8] We are independent

> "Those who are *dependent* need *permission* while the independent are always asking for forgiveness."

thinkers, workers, believers, fathers and mothers who at times need to be roped in by our wives, husbands, bosses, preachers and parents. We are like virtual storms spinning out at sea without any method to our madness. We are masters of persistence who come up with the most ludicrous ideas for getting things accomplished. Ideas like: How could I create something to fill nail holes in woodwork faster and more precisely? Enter the putty gun!

Those who are independent, increase at a much faster pace than those who are dependent. Those who depend on others tend to lean on technical achievement (not their own) as well as the ideas, actions and leadership of others. If direction is not clear from above, they will wait for it. They find it hard to make a judgment call and risk being wrong, and so they wait for commands to move forward. Those who are *dependent* need *permission* while the independent are always asking for *forgiveness*. The independent are far more results-oriented while the dependent are all about the process of gaining those results. This might explain why the results tend to be consistently out of reach for some.

The process is just the how of getting the result, but the independent know the result is the goal. With relentless fortitude they create it as fast as possible. We are bloodier, but we are happy. We depend on windfalls as opposed to planning a strategy. This is sick, but true. It's idiots like us who win the lottery[9] and are handsomely rewarded for being stupid. If you are an independent person, working to get your compliance up every now and then isn't a bad idea though. There's nothing worse than a low compliant person

8 I hate this saying, but I'm too impatient to think of another one.
9 I can count on two hands and two feet the amount of times I've played it.

who walks into a convenience store around Halloween. They gaze across the counter with milk for the kids, and suddenly see the new scratch ticket entitled, "Scary Rich." It takes discipline to walk away from that purchase.

The Gift of ADHD

ADHD (*Attention Deficit Hyperactivity Disorder*) is a beautiful thing. It's like being on LSD while working in a machine shop. Talk about the power of chance! My whole life has been about taking chances. Let me say something else about ADHD. It's at its peak while you are busy trying to get attention. The large downside is that you cannot pay attention during this process.

I'm not a doctor, but I live this. It's the High Influence disease. Me, myself and I are raiding the henhouse and we keep running into each other! I could go into the brainy method of discussion here, but what good would that do? All I know is that having ADHD has been akin to what the Bible calls the "*Great and terrible day of the Lord*."[10] It's both great and terrible, but the great outweighs the terrible by a long shot.

"ADHD causes a tremendous amount of energy that consistently needs to be expelled. If you learn to expel it in the right direction, you will become a rocket. If you expel it in every direction, you will be a hand grenade — not so much fun."

Having ADHD has allowed me to multitask like a freak. It has given me a very high degree of creativity and has allowed me to juggle many balls in the air for long periods of time.

It's like having your brain on steroids. The problems come when you have consistent starts and stops all the time. My wife has always said, "Thank God you don't believe Elvis is still alive or you would be dragging us all over East Oshkosh in order to find him!" She is right, I would be. Here's the deal, this is about accommodating all of

---

10 Joel 2:31 (KJV)

your ideas at once. I see attention deficit as a real plus because it's like being on speed.[11] ADHD causes a tremendous amount of energy that consistently needs to be expelled. you learn to expel it in the right direction, you will become a rocket. If you expel it in every direction, you will be a hand grenade — not so much fun.

For many, many years I performed more like buckshot. I expelled the energy in the right direction, but I had a wide open choke. My only hope was that one of those little bb's would hit a vital organ out there somewhere. I was more dependent upon the animal mistakenly getting in the way of my ammunition, as opposed to locking on the target with expert marksmanship! I knew that the senseless beast would have no chance in hell of survival if I could somehow actually hit one. What I have noticed though is that when I get focused on a task, I become a single bullet marksman.

When I first started college in 1981, I worked at a local Burger King[12] for minimum wage. By the end of the first year, my brother and I had invented a scheme known as "pre-closing."[13] I had learned the buying habits of each ethnic group within our city and determined the odds of how many would purchase in the final hour and a half. I would make the sandwiches and shakes to reflect my notions and then break down the machines one by one, cleaning them, and lining them with sandwich wrappings. When it came time to close, it was just a matter of throwing away the paper linings and cleaning the floors. We reduced the closing time from 2 hours to 7 minutes when we all did things in order. Eventually, the food inspector shut down our "pre-closing scheme" because of its unconventional approach and possibly for fear of some sort of reprisal.

Needless to say, other local BK's were negotiating with our store manager, trying to trade multiple workers in order to get my brother or me in their store because of our high-risk ability and ingenuity. The only way out of that job was for me to quit. My manager would sometimes send my co-worker Lucy and I to the movies — "on the clock" - to show his appreciation for our efforts! I could make a Whopper in less than 4 seconds. Lucy and I

---

11 I'm not advocating drug use here. Other than having taken steroids to gain weight, and the occasional glass of wine or beer, I've never taken a drug in my life.
12 This will go down in history as my all time favorite job.
13 Another ADHD invention.

could hold off an entire busload of students all by ourselves and not miss one sandwich.

I loved my job at Burger King. I made it fun. I had pet names for everyone. I decorated the bulletin board for Halloween. I would do tricks for sandwiches. I entertained the customers, and I made myself irreplaceable. I would even go fishing after midnight with the store manager. I eventually entertained the idea of attending BK University and becoming the best Burger King executive in the world. I was a bullet because I was focused on the task and I needed to be liked — a very powerful formula. Ahh… the glory days!

9

How to Glory in Weakness

The Power of Weakness

"All you need in this life is ignorance and confidence; then success is sure."
— MARK TWAIN

Punishing Virtue and Rewarding Vice

While attending seminary in Tulsa, OK in the mid 80's, I came upon some very interesting ideas that were foundational in forming some of my better theories. The theory I developed of punishing virtue and rewarding vice started in 1986 and came to fruition in 2004. The actual concept began with the Apostle Paul's thorn in the flesh narrative. In Second Corinthians, Paul writes about a vision he had and how he could not properly determine whether it took place in his mind or if it was an actual event. He just couldn't come to grips with which one it was and to this day theologians continue to speculate.[1]

What Paul believed is extremely informative here because it sets a framework for the virtue/vice concept I have created. Paul believed he was given from God a *thorn in the flesh*, an angel from Satan, to bring repeated

---

1 Whatever.

blows upon his life or flesh[2] (weird but true). Paul was convinced that whatever his trouble was, God approved of it and was not willing to take it from him under any circumstances. It is clear that Paul's' relationship with God enabled him to accept that God was in control of it. Whether God was or not is unclear to us and will continue to be the object of much speculation.

It is clear, however, that Paul didn't like it. This is evidenced by his overt references to it in his writings. In other words, he didn't let it go quietly. He claims to have asked God three times to do something about it and each time God's reply was, *"My grace is enough for you."*[3] Now here's the kicker — Paul changes his tune after his discussions with God to the point where he now boasts, glories and embraces his weaknesses. What was formally the enemy is suddenly his best friend. How did this happen? The first thing Paul realized is that his weaknesses promotes God's strengths both directly and indirectly. Secondly, he comes to grips with who he actually is as opposed to who he thought he was or wanted to be.

Here lies the key. People of Accidental Increase embrace both their strengths and weaknesses and see them both as strengths. The combination of my strengths and weaknesses is my single most powerful strength. What I am today is not only because of my strength, but also because of my weakness. Just knowing this brings great peace, but embracing it will bring success where failure once ruled the day. I have found that most of the people I deal with in regards to personality despise their weaknesses and see them as obstacles. This is not good "Ju-Ju."

There is tremendous power in knowing what you are not. If I know I'm not good with people, I won't feel bad when I don't get the promotion that requires people skills. This doesn't mean I don't try to increase my understanding about relationship building or attend a teamwork class, but rather I now have the fundamental building blocks to increase my ability in the area where I know I excel. This is a much more productive use of my time than working feverishly in the area that will always need attention.

We must set our affections on that which produces results rather than focusing our attention on that which does not. If you spend all your time playing to your weakness, you will become guilty of punishing your virtues

2 I think today we would call this a pain in the @!#$.
3 II Corinthians 12:9

and rewarding your vices. I remember attending a meeting where a vast majority of the attendees were late. The speaker waited for the latecomers and ignored those who were on time. Thus he punished those with virtue and rewarded those with vice. He did this because he couldn't get past the insecure feelings produced by speaking to a smaller group of people — a telltale sign he's actually in it for himself under the guise of being there for others.

This is our modern cultural shift and it's going to be the death of us if we do not stop it soon. You see it every day when the victim in a rape case is made out to look like the perpetrator because the defense attorney is more concerned with winning than he is with justice. Convoluted for sure. See Mumford's bird analogy.[4] It's no longer about truth any more — it's all about winning — another sign of a nation in free-fall. People with AI reward virtue and punish vice like it deserves.

The Power of Weakness

The power of weakness is much stronger than the power of strength. Those who increase capitalize on it. When speaking and conducting seminars, I always try to use myself as an example when dealing with "what not to do" issues. Fortunately, I have a wealth of instances to choose from… Like never pour gasoline on the brush pile in the backyard before lighting it because it could explode sky high and you might lose your eyebrows, singe the hair off your arms and almost die![5] Or never watch a seedy video in your underwear in the middle of the afternoon at home where your wife can walk in unannounced because she forgot the hotdogs.[6] Capitalize on your strengths and embrace your weaknesses. This is the formula for success hands down. If you recognize your weaknesses and agree with them, your adversaries can't hold you hostage by constantly heaping a generous helping of guilt upon your plate.

---

4 You know… flying in ever tightening circles until he becomes well acquainted with his colon.
5 This was right after graduating from Stupid School.
6 This stupid move turned out to be bad Ju-Ju. See chapter 7 for sorted details.

> "This is about raw character because when the charm wears off, all you have left is character."

Agree with your Adversary on the Way

Whenever the accuser's accusing voice hits my ears I say, "*You think that's bad, you should have been here yesterday when such and such happened… you'd have been proud of me!*" One of my favorite scriptures is Matthew 5:25 "*Settle matters quickly with your adversary who is taking you to court. Do it while you are still with him on the way or he may hand you over to the judge, and the judge may hand you over to the officer, and you may be thrown into prison.*"

You must be dead honest about your potential to be the most depraved human on the planet. Thinking you may be anything else will lead to the *satanic mind meld.*[7] Come to grips with it now and everything's downhill from here. You may be thinking that I'm providing licenses to sin, don't worry; you do enough of that without a license. This is about honesty, the foundation upon which integrity rests. Living a life of honesty will take you farther than charm and brains combined. This is about raw character because when the charm wears off, all you have left is character. I like to fight fire with a shower of cool refreshing water, not gasoline. The shower happens when we agree with our adversary on the way. Get used to saying this — "*Yes, I did that!*" Hiding things in the dark only delays the inevitable realization — that you have broken most, if not all of the 10 Commandments multiple times.

Weakness is not a negative. It's a positive times 10. Thinking that weakness is somehow disadvantageous is personal suicide at best and at worst, the fallout after the suicide has been successfully completed. Be a realist. This doesn't mean that you're the village idiot no one wants to be around. It means that you are truthful with yourself first, and then all those around you.

> "Just the other day my wife asked me, "*Why did you say that?*" I replied, "*I wanted you to think I was important.*"

---

7 When you end up convinced that you are better than you actually are. This is when the bottom falls out and your Christmas sled hits the dirt at about 55 miles per hour. You should try it sometime — not.

Just the other day my wife asked me, "*Why did you say that?*" I replied, "*I wanted you to think I was important.*" This was the truth and I'm so used to saying this, that it has become a family joke. Building your life around lies about whom you are or your advanced capabilities is like putting a second story on an empty lot.[8] Don't do it because it won't work.

The Island of Misfit Toys

This is where I lived for the first 16 years of my life. "*Nobody wants a Charlie in the box.*"[9] I didn't fit anywhere. I looked like a woman. I had a big nose (I broke it more than twice) and one good eye. I had no coordination. I had invisible friends and I believed in Santa until I was 12. The fact is we all are very critical of ourselves in life — especially when we are young and trying to fit in.

When I was about 13 or 14, I was vying for position within our youth group and trying desperately just to find my place. My sister was younger and wanted to fit in with an even deeper, more aggressive fervency. This created a competitive edge that I didn't understand at the time. My reactions to her led to winning first prize in the world's biggest idiot contest.[10] My sister was standing around a small group of kids I was pathetically trying to charm and in my warped opinion, was honing in on whatever attention I thought was left for me. That's when *it* happened. My sister got too close for comfort so I made some crude remark in order to embarrass her back to the house where she belonged. To my absolute dismay, she physically fought back and when I lifted my arm to push her away, she went careening down the stairs!

We were in a second story lobby and she nearly broke her leg to the horror of us all. She ended up destroying her kneecap and had to go to the hospital. She was laid up for quite some time… serves her right![11] Many of us have moments we would love to forget, but it's these very moments that have come to shape our lives. My sister and I are very close today despite this very need-oriented act of stupidity in the late 70's. Being a misfit is something

---

8 Just think about what this would look like for just a few minutes and then knock it off.

9 Quoted by the "Charlie-in-the-box" in *Rudolph The Red Nosed Reindeer*, 1964.

10 As if I wasn't already the favorite to win anyway.

11 This is one of the sickest things I have ever done. Maybe that's why she went into nursing…

I have learned to do well. To think I have gone from that pitiful moment by the stairs to consulting with the heads of multimillion-dollar companies seems ludicrous, but it is simply the mark of Accidental Increase.

One of the telltale signs that accompany those who dwell on the Island of Misfit Toys is that we don't know what to do with our lives. We may know what we want, but we can't seem to find our way there with much clarity. In the infamous made for TV Special *Rudolph The Red Nosed Reindeer*, Hermey[12] wanted to be a dentist, but he was stuck being an elf.

As the show progresses, Hermey finds his destiny as a dentist while Rudolph finds himself and his first love. Rudolph is able to capitalize on his freakish light up nose, which is what makes him a misfit to begin with. It's weird how Santa almost appears to be a bigoted, wacko racist in this short animation. After all, he actually eliminates Rudolph from the sleigh team just because Rudolph is different. It sure made the point though.

Much like Rudolph, the best part of being a late bloomer is that we are great bloomers once we finally come of age. I started blooming in my 30's. Before that, I was just a blooming idiot. This is true for a lot of people. It takes us that long to figure out who we are (as well as who we are not). And like Hermey, it's through much adversity that we eventually discover ourselves. If you're blooming late, then just relax. Your day will come and come it will! It'll probably hit you like a bad accident.

A Perfect Fit

A misfit is a person who is not suited or able to adjust to the circumstances of his or her particular situation in life. Once these circumstances change though, many misfits become perfect fits. Like Hermey, misfits often are merely victims of bad environments or circumstances.[13] Paul Potts was is a former misfit who now travels the world dazzling people with his gifted voice. He's even performed for the queen of England! All that misfits need is the correct environment, job or circumstance and they are no longer held hostage by bad circumstantial weirdness. Everyone has a place in this world

---

12 The original scripts do not say Herbie as you might believe. Premiering on NBC December 6th, 1964, RUDOLPH has become the longest running, highest rated television special in the history of the medium.
13 A dentist stuck wearing an elf suit at the North Pole is a real bummer.

— it's just that some people are out of that place for the moment. I have seen scores of different people find love, work and joy when the circumstances were just right. The problem is not with the person. It's when the person and the right circumstances fail to align that brings the misfortune. People are generally great, except for the few maniacs who make their way into town now and again.

Understand that once the right situation arises, you will thrive in it, but until then, it may feel like you are just surviving. I still have googley eyes[14] and an oversized nose, but at least I no longer look like a woman thank God! Life has created the right dynamics to where I now thrive in it. For many years this was not so, but how I responded during those years has enabled me to have the proper EQ and attitude to make the most of the years ahead. My whole history is part of the process God has used to bring me to this point. I love the future!

Embracing Your Weakness

Embracing your weakness means that you embrace all the things about yourself that you deem to be liabilities. Think of yourself as a battery. You must have both the *positive* and the *negative* to ensure success. It's supposed to be this way! Your ability comes from the combination of the two, which in turn creates your genius! You just have to make the right connection!

Everyone has something to offer. Don't forget that. A man by the name of Owen Feltham once said, "The greatest results in life are usually attained by simple means and the exercise of ordinary qualities. These may for the most part be summed in these two: common-sense and perseverance." You got it… good ole' horse sense.

"Embracing your weakness means that you embrace all the things about yourself that you deem to be liabilities. Think of yourself as a battery. You must have both the *positive* and the *negative* to ensure success."

---

14 I put a nail through my left eye when I was about 10 years old and so it's crooked now.

Albert Einstein said, *"Try not to be a man of success, but a man of value."* People of value tend to do more by accident than what people of material success do on purpose. Value is determined by what's on the inside. Remember the particleboard example from Chapter 1? Why we paint particleboard and varnish oak? We paint to conceal. We varnish because we appreciate the beauty as well as the flaws of great wood and we don't try to hide it.

Eric Moussambani[15] won brief international fame at the 2000 Summer Olympics when he swam his heat of the 100-meter freestyle in 1:52.72. This was a terrible time for an Olympic swimmer by the way. Moussambani had gained entry to the Olympics without meeting the minimum qualification requirements via a wildcard draw designed to encourage developing countries (without expensive training facilities) to participate. He won the heat because the two other competitors were disqualified for making false starts. *He had only learned to swim less than a year earlier!*

Moussambani's fame spread, not because of what he could do, but because of what he could not do! He flailed in the water like a crippled fish during the last few meters but received a standing ovation because he didn't quit! He will go down in history as the world's worst, best swimmer! It was his perseverance that qualified him for greatness!

"I saw it on TV like everyone else and it was quite amazing the cheer that he got swimming that race," said Ian Thorpe, who had already won three swimming gold medals at the 2000 Games. *"That was quite incredible. And that's what the Olympics are about. Athletes from around the world having the opportunity to swim at the biggest event there is."*

This is a prime example of Accidental Increase happening before your very eyes. There are plenty of videos on YouTube of Moussambani's performance to inspire you and challenge you towards your own destiny. Be grateful for what you have and for who you are. Nothing can stop you from capitalizing on either your strengths or your weaknesses as Moussambani did. He became famous for his outer weakness, solely because of his *inner* strength. He took full advantage of his battery!

---

15 Nicknamed "Eric The Eel" after the name first appeared in an article by Craig Lord in *The Times* newspaper in London.

10

Self Deception

The Power of De-Nile

"*Patterning your life around other's opinions is nothing more than slavery.*"
— LAWANA BLACKWELL

Swimming down De-Nile

In all my life, one characteristic that has always baffled me is the ability some people have to deny the reality of their actual state of being. The capacity to tell yourself rational lies has got to be either the greatest gift on this earth or the greatest poison ever mixed. Swimming down De-Nile is so much easier than swimming up De-Truth. I should know. As an expert swimmer, I can honestly say that one of my strongest suits is to recognize rational lies before they take hold of me. If I decide to defy my conscience, it's with full intention on my part. Seconds before a violation, the voice of conscience will scream within me and I will hear it as clear as anything. To proceed with the violation will be outright evil intent on my part with zero excuses to follow. This has been my lot in life since childhood.

People of Accidental Increase always see things as they are, not as they want them to be. In the mid-1800s, a European doctor by the name of Ignaz Semmelweis (pronounced "Ignawtz Semelvice") made a horrific discovery that would change the world, as we know it. He worked in Vienna's General Hospital as an obstetrician. Semmelweis had a very appalling problem. The mortality rate in his section of the ward was one-in-ten births. Imagine out of every ten babies you had one dying under your custody and supervision. Woman around Vienna were so frightened that many would rather give birth in the street than to allow the hospital to lend its caring hand.

Although completely obsessed with this problem, Semmelweis was unable to find out why 'childbed fever' was so prevalent within his ward. Eventually, through a series of trials and errors a discovery was made. This fantastic discovery became known as the germ. You see the General Hospital was a teaching and research hospital. Semmelweis would split his time between working on cadavers and working on young mothers to be — yikes! Unfortunately, many children went to an early grave because Semmelweis didn't know he had a problem. Self-deception acts the very same way.

We tend to our business with eagerness and expectation, unaware of the many issues that invade us. We are self-deceived. I say "self" because we shouldn't be surprised that the fickle finger of fate points right back at us. The Apostle James wrote about this very thing in his Epistle when he said, *"Do not merely listen to the word and so deceive yourselves. Do what it says."*[1] This is good and true advice. How often have we quoted the words of Solomon and others in an attempt to rescue someone else, when all the while we are rowing with mighty gusto towards the same waterfall?

As a consultant and behavioral analyst, I work with managers and leaders all the time. From time to time, I will put a group of subordinates through what is called a "360" assessment of the very leader they serve. This assessment is created by me and reflects the necessary leadership dynamics needed for this particular team to grow and learn under their leader. Each employee is responsible to measure his or her leader's management ability, Emotional Intelligence and skills while remaining anonymous. The leader or

---

1 James 1:22

manager also participates in this exercise, rating themselves on how they see their own leadership prowess.

Nearly every single time I have performed this process, I see the same identical outcome. The leaders almost always rate themselves higher than their subordinates rate them. This is what is known as a blind spot. By nature, we tend to see ourselves more favorable than what is reality. This is the self-preservation principle. Those who Accidentally Increase consistently see themselves more clearly than those who don't. I remember an incident that took place in the early 90s when I got myself in a compromising position because I willingly violated my screaming conscience. The people I interacted with after the incident looked at me in near disbelief. They couldn't recall the last time they dealt with anyone so *honest* about themselves or so *willing* to take responsibility for their actions. Funny, I thought it was the norm.

I have plenty of faults my friend, but lying to myself has never been one of them. Solomon said, *"Buy the truth and sell it not..."*[2] what a simple yet profound statement. Do not be one who lives in self-deception. Successful people take responsibility for their actions. I'm always amazed by people who shirk responsibility. Have you ever had an individual damage something while working in your home? Don't you just love it when they say, "It was like that?" Give yourself the gift of truth and you will never be the same.

I recall years ago power washing some decks for someone and inadvertently bleaching someone else's deck chairs. Those in charge of the operation insisted, "Steve would never do that" when the irate customer complained about the incident. When challenged by the condo authority, I told them it was entirely possible that I could have done it. I told them I would take full responsibility for the mishap, I went back to the residence, knocked on the person's door and said, *"I'm the one who probably ruined your deck chairs."* They couldn't believe my honesty. They invited me in and showed me around the house. Next they handed me a drink, invited me to a party and said, *"Don't worry about it."* I made an instant friend. Could you imagine if I had said, *"it was like that?"* — Yuck!

One of my favorite new sayings is this; *"You will never go wrong going right."*[3] This is so true. You cannot lose when taking responsibility and being

2 Proverbs 23:23 (KJV)
3 I came up with this in 2007.

honest about who you are and who you are not. Losing is for liars, cheats and manipulators. Don't be a loser. Years ago, I was working with a partner[4] of sorts and had purchased a new (used) vehicle for work. I had to schedule an appointment to get the registration and insurances together before I could put it into service. We were so busy though that it slipped my mind and we were driving the truck without the proper paperwork. My partner didn't know it, but for some reason he just flat out asked me about it one day.

"*So you finally got all the paperwork done, huh?*" I immediately responded, "*Yes*" without any hesitation, but in that nano-second realized I was outright lying out of fear of being an idiot for taking so long. I kept this moronic secret for about 6 hours before breaking the terrible news, to my own demise.

"I lied to you this morning," I said.
"What? You didn't register the truck?"
"No. I didn't."
"You idiot. Let's just go get mine then," and it was over.
"Why did you lie to me about that?" he said.
"I was afraid you would think I was an idiot," I said.
"You are," he replied.

We laugh our heads off about it now, but at the time I felt pretty stupid. Here's the thing; I was being stupid. In fact, I was being a first class moron. But what I wasn't doing was trying to wiggle out of it. I wasn't rationalizing the problem. I hit it head on and was completely truthful. My lie was defensive but not defrauding and I came clean, albeit 6 hours later. This is not an attempt to excuse the behavior, but an attempt to show you that we all have our moments of glory[5]. Moments when we're standing in the living room in our underwear with a stupid look on our face.

Plate Glass and Panes

A woman once asked me, "*Can you give me any gambling verses in the Bible?*" I told her that while I wasn't aware of any specifics, I was more

---

4 Jack Myatt is a dear friend who taught me most of what I know about business, which isn't much.
5 Or perhaps, moments of gory.

interested in knowing why she wanted the information in the first place. She replied that she had a friend who played the state lottery from time to time. She was hoping for some ammunition to point out to her friend the error of her way. Bing! This was when I discovered my blood had a boiling point.

"*Have you ever told a lie?*" I asked her directly.
"*Why of course,*" she replied.
"*Then let's find some text that refers to your sad situation instead because we have plenty of it,*" I said.

She didn't understand at first, so I had to bring her up to speed on the matter. From what I could gather, she viewed life as a stained-glass window with many panes. Thus to miss the mark in life was equivalent to throwing a rock through one of those panes. Because she took notice that her friend had some broken panes, she was about to load up her arsenal and bust her friend for having a broken window. You might have called her the *window police*.[6]

Back to life — Back to Reality

The Apostle James brings us back to reality in his Epistle when he says, "*For whoever keeps the whole law and yet stumbles at just one point is guilty of breaking all of it.*"[7] There are no individual panes in this life, only plate glass windows. If you put a small pebble through any part of the glass, the whole window will be damaged and in need of replacement.

This situation is either/or. You are either able to keep your window whole or you are not — period. Many people like to check everyone else's windows to see which panes are broken. If they see a broken pane in an area of life where they have found freedom, they are quick to criticize and offer their solution. There was a time when I thought I was the chief window inspector

"People of *Accidental Increase* do not inspect other people's glass. They see it as a mirror to themselves."

6 Or perhaps a pane in the glass!
7 James 2:10

> "People of increase see themselves as they really are and deal honestly with it. They don't blame others for their own failures."

of the universe. Thankfully, that time has ended. People of *Accidental Increase* do not inspect other people's glass. They see it as a mirror to themselves.

James claims *"mercy triumphs over judgment."*[8] He writes that we should speak and act as those who are going to be judged by the law that gives freedom! I suggest you and I take James' advice seriously. We can either criticize or we can intercede for others. People of Accidental Increase are those who know their faults and limitations. They treat others with respect and dignity. They are lovers of those within this world. If they are going to make a judgment, it begins at home where they live. St. Paul writes that we should judge ourselves first, lest we be *condemned* with the world.[9] People of increase see themselves as they really are and deal honestly with it. They don't blame others for their own failures.

A Problem from the Beginning

When you think about it, this whole throwing others under the bus routine has been going on for a long, long time. Way back in the Genesis narrative, we read that after Adam lost control of his family, he blamed his wife. This was the wife that God had personally handcrafted for him. Adam couldn't take responsibility for failing to lead properly. When God confronted Eve, she blamed the serpent and failed to take personal responsibility for her actions just as Adam did earlier in the story. This was a large part of their sin. This story illustrates why the greatest part of repentance is taking personal responsibility for ones' actions, and the greater part of sinfulness is failing to do so. We all miss the mark, but few of us are willing to take responsibility for it. David, a man after God's own heart, got it right. After David committed adultery and then had the husband murdered, the prophet Nathan called David out on the carpet.

---

8 James 2:13
9 1 Corinthians 11:31

"*It is against you alone Oh Lord that I have sinned*," was King David's reply. Oh, that we could all recognize that, and deal with God directly and instantly, instead of passing the buck. Someone told me early on in my adult life; "*If you are quick to repent and quick to forgive, you will always make it.*"[10]

To Know Me is to Love Me

Years ago, there was a phrase that floated around rather frequently. "To know me is to love me" is what it said. This is perhaps the biggest difference between God and man. He knows us and still loves us.

When I went on my first date with Anita who is now my wife, I was dead set on being myself. I didn't want her to fall in love with a fake. I took her to a fine restaurant. During our time there, I was laughing, making jokes, burping and balancing the saltshaker atop the catsup bottle. I was being *me*!

She later told me it was the most comfortable she had ever been on a dinner date. Today I am the same person I was on that night 25 years ago. There has never been a mask. What she saw is what she got — period. She still has it today. Accidental Increase takes place when we are honest and real.

Many people today want to keep things in the closet and not reveal them for various reasons. This is a great way to stay addicted to stupid pills. One of the reasons why we fail to be real is because we simply do not like who and what we are. We believe that the image we portray is the more acceptable image and we hide our *true* selves in the closet. Unfortunately, we can't stay in the closet very long. About 6 months to a year into the marriage, out we come in all our glory. Once we feel comfortable, the mask slowly and deliberately begins to fall.

This is usually when things go south, something neither one of us signed up for. All too often this is the case in our culture today. People are selfish and concerned with self more than they are with the person they married. We are in control of who will bring what to our table. Rarely do we look at a relationship to see what we can add to it. We must be completely open and honest with people if we are going to experience true success.

Years ago, I was looking to purchase the home I was renting because I had first right of refusal on the property. Two individuals owned the property

---

10 The late Kenneth E. Hagin told me this in 1987.

and I was pretty friendly with both. One of the owners was willing to sell for about $70,000 less than the other individual. This created quite a problem within my cranium as you might imagine.[11] After all, no one wants to spend more than they have to. I was limited on the amount I could purchase the home for and so I began to panic and fear that I would miss the opportunity to buy. Many of those who knew I wanted to purchase the home would inquire as to how it was going.

This is when I began to whine and complain to anyone who would offer solace to my situation. *Self-pity always agrees with you.* Unfortunately, word got out that one of the owners was *"stiffing"* the Sisler's. I didn't know this rumor was circulating until the other owner phoned me one day.

"So and so is pissed! Did you say thus and such about him? You'd better fix it, bro!"

This was never my intention nor was I even aware that this had taken place! During the phone conversation, I could *feel* the blood draining from my face and I felt like I had just downed a bucket of mud.
"I'll make it right," I said to the owner on the phone. I immediately phoned the other individual who was so angry with me he could hardly speak. We agreed to meet at a location and hash it out within the hour. My adrenalin began to run wild. I felt like I had just graduated top of my class from Idiot School for the Insane. What was I going to do? We met and he just stared at me with daggers in his eyes. He began to explain his side of the story including what he had heard. His eyes were flooded and he was red in the face. If I had not known him, I would have feared an altercation on some level. I had created a volcano.

When he finished what he needed to say, I just looked at him and said, "It's all true." I looked him dead in the eye and said, *"I panicked and I was afraid. Can you find it in your heart to forgive me?"* He did. He was a man of character. That pretty much ended the conversation right there. I went home and drafted a letter of apology to every single person I might have spoken to and explained that I was just being a scared fool and the picture I inadvertently painted was very wrong and misleading. I asked them to forgive me as well.[12]

---

11 This triggered some pretty weird thought processes.
12 And they all did... imagine that!

I sent the letters out that very day and mailed one to the owner I misrepresented explaining what I was doing. At this point, getting the house was no longer the goal. Repairing the damaged relationship was now *top* priority for me. *Relationships are primary, not instrumental,* and I was the agent in my own experiment. To be honest, I forgot about the house during this time and only concentrated on taking my medicine. Several weeks later I got a call and they were both willing to sell at my asking price. We are still friends to this day.

"People of increase see themselves as they really are and deal honestly with it. They don't blame others for their own failures."

This is not about living perfectly folks. It's about being *real*[13] and living up to what you claim about yourself. It's about looking in the mirror and being able to say, "*You just acted like a blooming idiot; now go fix your mess!*" This isn't about *if* we screw up, it's about what we are going to do *when* we screw up.

Accidental Increase comes when we take *full* responsibility for our every action no matter how stupid it is. Is there someone you need to meet with this week? If so, take a hard moral inventory, then suit up and get it over with. You've got so much more living and giving to do then to get stuck in that awful place. Breathe the free air my friend, and let others drink from your fountain of humility.

---

13 As opposed to a big lying jerk.

11

The Incredible Robot Experiment

The Power of Ownership

"My life has no purpose, no direction, no aim, no meaning, and yet I'm happy. I can't figure it out. What am I doing right?"
— CHARLES M. SCHULZ

Owning your Ideas

The psychologist Jonathan Freedman conducted an experiment with elementary school children in 1965 that produced some astounding results. Freedman was anxious to see if he could prevent second to fourth grade boys from playing with a robot toy. He specifically wanted to note the type of behavior he would have to employ to keep the children occupied and away from "BB Sputnik."

Without going into all the details surrounding the experiment, this is basically what took place. Twenty-two boys were individually placed inside a small room with five toys. Four of the toys were extremely boring while one toy (the robot) was to be coveted. Before Freedman allowed each boy into the room to play with the toys, he threatened the child with punishment if he touched the toy robot. A second group was brought in with this one difference. In the second trial group, the severe threat of punishment was replaced with a mild threat that invited the boy's participation to not engage with the robot.

Here's what happened. Under the severe threat, 21 boys avoided playing with the robot altogether. Under the lesser threat (just stating that it is wrong to touch the robot), 21 boys avoided the robot as well. The experiment was not over. Six weeks later, Freedman sent a woman back to the school to administer a short written test to the two groups of boys. While the test was being corrected, both groups of boys were put into the room with the same 5 toys but this time without any threat at all.

An amazing thing happened. Out of the original trial group (under the severe threat) 77% chose to play with the formerly forbidden toy. The severe threat had virtually no impact on the boys' behavior. In contrast, out of those who were mildly threatened, only 33% chose to play with the once taboo toy. This is was a very interesting experiment, which helped prove some theories.

Threats don't work! When we threaten to punish, the unwanted actions are put aside until the threat is gone, but the person has not actually taken ownership of the idea at all. As soon as the threat is removed, the unwanted action is enacted and the unwanted behavior continues without hesitation.

The reason the second group of boys displayed a lesser amount of playing with the robot is simple. They owned the idea. Because there was virtually no threat initially, the idea to obey was created by the child on the first experimental study. When the children were brought into the toy room the second time, they still owned the original idea and therefore didn't play with the forbidden toy. People of Accidental Increase own their ideas. Like the children in the second experiment, they live up to that which they own. Conversely, you will live down to that which you don't.

Owning your ideas is one of the most important strategies for accomplishment. In the 16th chapter of Luke's Gospel, the Christ explains that if you are faithful with that which belongs to someone else, it will qualify you to have your own. When I was faithful with my friend's business in the late 80's, it qualified me to have my own business less than 3 years later. You must own your ideas if they are going to work for you. Just having an idea is pointless and it will produce nothing. Owning the idea will bring creative approaches to making it a reality. The reason why so many within the workforce do not live up to their ability at work is because they don't own their job — it belongs to the owner. The result? They work for the weekend instead.

Creating Ownership in Others

The way we create ownership in others is to discipline, as opposed to punish, wrongful behavior. Punishing is when we make our children pay for inconveniencing us. When a child embarrasses a parent at the local eatery, many times the parent will punish the child for making them look like a fool in public. This really has nothing to do with the child and everything to do with the parent.

Most parents believe that a child's behavior is somehow a reflection of their ability to raise and nurture the child. Most of the time this is not true, especially when the child is young and testing the boundaries. Only when the child becomes older does the reflection model come into play and even then it is limited. Most children are just acting like children. When we punish a child because the child "made us look ridiculous," we are not teaching the child anything about life, but rather, we are making the child pay for the damages. This is judgment. We make the judgment and then carry out the proper sentencing and often throw away the key.

Discipline is altogether different. The word itself comes from the word disciple, meaning disciplined learner. When we discipline a child, it is for the child's welfare at parental expense. Discipline takes much more work and patience to pull off. You have to talk things through and make sense. You have to help the child own the idea of new behaviors for a reason, not just because you say so. It takes time and tremendous emotional intelligence to reason with a child.

> "When we punish a child because the child "*made us look ridiculous,*" we are not teaching the child anything about life, but rather, we are making the child pay for the *damages.*"

You have to spell out the reasons why the behavior is harmful to them as opposed to you. That takes some doing. You also have to sell the idea as opposed to tell the idea. Telling the idea is forcing them to buy whereas selling the idea invites them into the process and creates a *"want to"* within the child. Once the child wants too, they will continue to do so. The same goes for employees within a company or organization. Good managers create environments where employees can own ideas. Poor managers shout orders and create dissonance among subordinates. Sadly, this latter approach is more popular than the former.

It takes personal sacrifice to create great people who can own great ideas. Where on this earth did we get the idea that people have their act together? We only dilute ourselves into thinking that way because we don't take the time to invest in others.

Looking Out For Number One

Every new environment calls for training and adaptation on the part of both parties. You should never stop investing in people, especially your children. Parenting is the toughest job that you'll ever have. There is plenty of written material, but children come with their own set of instructions that takes a lifetime to figure out! Whether creating children, employees or soldiers, all require *five* stages to maximize the results. They are *recruit, train, deploy, monitor* and *nurture*. Most companies simply want to recruit and deploy. They forget about training, monitoring and nurturing. That's why so many companies operate like a three-ring circus. Great people are crafted. Great people have to be trained to be great. The training period is the place of investment!

Paying someone to learn something creates a dynamic that is absent in most people's lives. You are giving them knowledge and money. In the case of your children, they are receiving knowledge, food and shelter. You get nothing during the training period as a leader, parent or manager! This is the period of time where the employee or child is the receiver and you are the giver. Within families, from age 1 to 18 you are investing for free! It is usually not until the child is about 30 that you begin to reap the rewards of great parenting. This training period produces loyalty, self-assurance, and dignity within the child, or employee. Human nature will typically enact the reciprocity principle during this time. This means that there is now a built in determination and drive to pay back the giver.

"When you *don't* take the time to train people, you create a *survival* instinct in them that causes them to act in a way that preserves and protects self."

When you don't take the *time* to train people, you create a *survival* instinct in them that causes them to act in a way that preserves and protects *self*. This is always at the expense of everyone around them. They have been trained to look out for number one, and you trained them. Blame yourself first and then work to remedy your mistakes. If you made a set of bad decisions, there is always time to make a different one in the right direction.

I believe many people are survivors simply because they had to emotionally raise themselves. This is true within a company and it's also true within the home. Accidental Increase takes place when your home life is fairly healthy. It will also take place in you as you provide that healthy atmosphere. People shouldn't be simply surviving — they should be thriving!

You can also Accidentally Increase if you have managed to survive well even though your situation was not necessarily the best one. If you have played your cards right it will produce good things, regardless of how bad the cards were that you were dealt with.

I Told You So

"Papa don't preach, I'm in trouble deep, Papa don't preach, I've been losing sleep, But I made up my mind, I'm keeping my baby."

Released by Madonna in June of 1986, the song Papa Don't Preach[1] quickly rose to the top of the pop charts, becoming Madonna's fourth number-one single. The song's lyrics and subject matter created quite a stir at the time. It also became the source of much conflict between Madonna and

1 Written by Brian Elliot and produced by Stephen Bray.

the Vatican, when she dedicated it to Pope John Paul II. Like a stone thrown into a pond of calm water, the ripple effects were pretty spectacular.

To its credit though, the song addresses several controversial subjects in a very unique manner. It deals directly with teenage pregnancy and the abortion issue, as well as the unwed mother phenomenon. It also makes a rather pointed reference to the young girl's father. Instead of loving her through the process, her father demonstrates an "I told you so" attitude.

The girl's response is to reject her father but accept her child. I realize that this song is a "fictional dilemma," but we need to understand that people are going to make mistakes — big, bad, ugly mistakes.

"To err is human, to forgive divine."[2]

Does God have grace for you? Then you need to have grace for others who find themselves jumping from the plane without a parachute. Instead of becoming part of the problem, work hard at loving people. People of increase do not have an *"I told you so"* attitude. Jesus didn't. He hated the problems but loved the people.

Investing as a Way of Life

Self-awareness, no matter how painful, in the end becomes the qualifier for great deeds. When the image of ourselves remains either marred or poor, two things result; an inability to properly invest in other people and an inability to enjoy making that investment. Broken vessels cannot hold water.

"Courageous people invest in others because the absence of self demands it."

We must accept our repairs and make ourselves useful during the process. The inability to embrace our brokenness is both harmful and selfish. Courageous people invest in others because the absence of self demands it.

When we spend all our time gazing at ourselves in the rearview mirror instead of looking out in front of us, we ultimately end up

2 Alexander Pope, An Essay on Criticism. English poet & satirist (1688 - 1744).

crashing the car. If you look inquisitively within the Gospel narratives, you will find a man who invested in the lower end of society at the total expense of his own life. His name is Jesus. He thus becomes the poster-boy of all future investors in the human condition. His ability to invest himself in others (apart from his divine mission as the savior of the world) was derived from a single source of energy. That energy was love; love for his father God, love of self and love for others.

Knowing and loving God the Father through both relationship and revelation brought about an understanding of tremendous proportions. This enlightenment became the driving force behind his cause and his mission. As his understanding of his father broadened, the results were reflected in his understanding of self and ultimately of others. It is therefore impossible to define self and/or others apart from defining God. It is imperative that this be understood.

Jesus' famous words, *"not my will, but yours be done"*[3] serve as a backdrop for successful relationship maneuvering. When we cease focusing on our own needs, opportunities for helping others become more evident. Because of the power behind the self-preservation principle, selfish behavior tends to be the natural outcome in the human order. If you're like me, you didn't have to invest in any books or tapes on the subjects of lies and deceptions in order to help your children along with their early behavioral dynamics. Lying was an automatic response to preserve our position in the family.

There are two kinds of *lies*, lying to defend and lying to defraud. [4] As a defensive tactic, lying becomes a transitive verb describing the need to protect or defend self from harm, attack or danger. This is more instinctive as it relates to the human condition. My son Matty lied about eating my chocolate kisses once. He wasn't being deceptive, he was being protective. I just carried him over to the bathroom mirror and allowed him to see the rewards all over his little face. I didn't punnish him, I just told him to eat his own candy. He was about four. Don't be idiotic with your kids.

Defrauding however, is meant to *deprive* another through dishonest means in an attempt to gain for self the things we believe are rightfully ours when they are not. This type of lie does not emit from a sense of need, but

---

3 Luke 22:42
4 Each of my children would be disciplined differently - depending on which type they told.

rather from a sense of want or entitlement. Therefore, when we focus on another person in an attempt to consider them first, (not my will, but yours) the lying principle is dropped from the equation altogether.

Own your own life. Be responsible. Invest in other people. Like the children who made a conscious decision to keep away from the robot toy because they believed it was the right thing to do, so also you need to make a conscious decision. Decide who you are, what you will do and why you will do it. Land your plane right now. Is there someone you have been withholding love or information from? Do you have a child that is difficult to love? An employee? The decision is yours.

12

One Common Language

The Power of Communication

"I have learned, that if one advances confidently in the direction of his dreams, and endeavors to live the life he has imagined, he will meet with a success unexpected in common hours."

— HENRY DAVID THOREAU

Universal Communication

There is a universal language we communicate. Although we may not be completely aware of it, we are communicating with everyone around us whether we like it or not. These cues are known as "observable indicators" and those who increase tend to watch for these vital signs. Have you ever been speaking to someone when you suddenly realize that no one is home? Perhaps it was a wandering eye, a blank stare, or a "just a minute, I've got to take this call." These indicators, behaviors observed or calculated, are used to show the presence or state of mind within that particular individual. They are both universal and dependable in their inherent ability to communicate exactly what the individual is feeling internally. We can pick up silent messages, which are being sent via behavioral patterns, and understand what an individual is saying and usually, without them uttering a single word.

People Reading

The ability to "people read," becomes an important tool for understanding what some are unable to express verbally and those who Accidentally Increase know how to do it. Mastering this technique makes you a master communicator. The ability to understand and receive messages is at times, more important than your ability to send them. Understanding this basic idea of communication is foundational in our approach to understanding each other in a more mature manner.

The people reading process, as powerful as it may be, also has its limitations. Intelligence, education, training, experience and skill sets are all areas that the people reading process will not uncover. The behavioral indicators that are transferred through the people reading process is the "how" of a person's behavior, not the "why" of that behavior. The "why" of an individual's behavior is limited to the value sector covered in the first chapter... Even though the "why" segment of the individual is measurable; it is not measurable through the "observables." The observables — that which comes through seeing or noticing something, only deal with the "how" factor.

The language of "how we act" or the "language of actions" is one of the oldest languages in the world. What makes this language so unique is the fact that everyone can learn the language, and that the language is universally spoken without biases. This "cross cultural" language is miraculously accurate no matter where you may be. Russians, Japanese, Spanish, Israelis, and Americans all speak and understand this language universally. As an obvious example, think of how easy it might be to communicate that you are hungry or thirsty to people that don't speak your native language. Taking the time to read someone is paramount when interacting on any level deeper than an acquaintance. Those who increase have an ability to look past superficial actions and see the meaning behind them. This is a learned ability, which could become extremely profitable if you take the time to acquire it.

Most people generally ignore tone of voice, signs of impatience and other cues in their hurried attempt to get a conversation focused back on themselves. Don't be one of them. Your failure to read the cues given by others will always result in a collision of some sort. Become a master of behavioral cues and you will not only increase your brainpower, you will also increase your horse sense.

Word, Gesture and Spirit

We communicate through three fundamental avenues — word, gesture and spirit.[1] All of these are observable in one form or another. Our words are observable through the listening process, by the person who listens. Words have two possible outcomes when received by another. These words either give life or take it. Anyone who has ever been on the receiving end of a killer word knows this. "Stupid," "moron," "idiot" and "loser" are all killer words. Accompanied by a spirit of hurt with macabre gestures, and these words do their job quite well.

Those who *Accidentally Increase* find ways to maximize words that build and minimize those that destroy. When we speak words in the spirit of healing with accompanying gestures, they build up and make people alive. Ask any child who has been beaten down by cruel words and gestures about how things are going. Look into their eyes, and you can actually see the pain. We are communicating all the time. Therefore it is imperative to not only be aware of what we are saying, but also how we are saying it.

Gestures are actions that communicate negative and positive cues. When a person smiles it can brighten another's day and give them strength to move ahead. A wink, a nod or any small token gesture can be the turning point in someone's life, pivotal if not crucial in many. We must be aware of the impact that gestures make in the communication process. The negative is true as well. Slamming doors and heavy breathing are indicators that we have not

> "Those who *Accidentally Increase* find ways to maximize words that build and minimize those that destroy."

---

1 This concept was originally taught by the late Edwin Louise Cole.

forgiven nor have we forgotten what someone has done to us. Our cues are communicating the fact that we are holding another in the prison of inconvenience and dissatisfaction. Many years ago my daughter (she was about 4 years old) violated the rule of leaving the designated boundary line that surrounded our home. This boundary had been effectively communicated by us and was understood by her. Her love for animals helped her over our safety net on that particular day. She had followed a neighborhood dog out of the yard and across several streets as well as negotiating an empty swimming pool! You can imagine the horror her mother and I experienced once we discovered her missing. During the disciplinary moment I explained the situation as it stood and allowed her to choose the disciplinary action. The choices were either *no date with daddy* or a *spanking on the bum*. She just looked up at me and started to cry. When I asked her why she was crying, she proceeded to tell me that she only had one option...the spanking. She just could not miss the date with daddy.

After the spanking was over, I picked her up in my arms and held her tight against my chest and assured her of my undying love for her. It was then that we went out for our date and I never brought up the incident again. I did not hold her hostage to the former moments of violation by giving her subtle cues relaying my disappointments. She never left the yard again.

Communicating through spirit is a bit more illusive, but it is the most powerful of the three. I once heard a story of a boy who was diagnosed with a mental disorder and was subsequently sent to the doctor for evaluation. The doctor interviewed the boy's mother as well as the boy himself. After several weeks of institutionalization and evaluation, the boy's mother was asked to come take him home. When the boy's mother walked into the room to receive her son, the boy cowered into the arms of the doctor. The doctor was surprised because the boy's mother was smiling and seemed excited to receive the boy back. When the doctor asked the boy why he was afraid, he replied, "she's happy with her face but she is mad in her eyes." The boy knew he was headed back to a dysfunctional environment and his mother's spirit revealed it. The communicative process is an important part of human development and understanding. It is necessary for life and love. The necessity of mastering its process is essential. People of increase are onto it.

Conflict Resolution

Someone once said, "Misunderstanding is the foundation underneath every conflict." Indeed, most of our relational problems stem from misunderstanding the motives, actions and behaviors of others. We also tend to be negative by nature. Recognizing this and then making a concerted effort to be positive will help create an environment of successful relationship opportunity.

People are naturally against what they fail to understand. Gaining an understanding of the differences between yourself and others is the first of many steps toward conflict resolution. When we take the time to really get to know someone, we are showing him or her that we care about them. If we take the time to "people read," we will learn more about them in 12 minutes than we otherwise could in a whole year.

This is how we diffuse problems before they begin. In our fast-paced society, we are too busy to "figure people out." Take the 12 minutes to people read your prospect. You will gain a tremendous amount of insight that will be useful to you for years to come. Eliminating conflict makes for longtime relationships, easier navigation, and smoother transitions with those whom we associate with every day. If you are going to increase the power of your relationships, learn about those you love and those who you are trying to love.

Communicating through Touch

The power of touch is something we are becoming less and less familiar with in this culture. Those who practice Accidental Increase are masters of touch. I entered a men's room a few days ago and I didn't have to touch anything. I didn't touch the toilet (thank God), the towels or the faucet. All I touched was the water and the soap. I think part of our cultural problem today is the lack of appropriate touch. We're becoming a touch-free society. I was in the airport the other day and noticed a great advertisement in one of the terminals. It was a little sign on the wall showing a woman whispering sweet nothings into a gentleman's ear. The caption read, "The original instant message." What a great advertising campaign!

With the advent of the electronic message, we are moving away from the original instant messaging system- touching. Touch, a significant component of traditional healing, is being increasingly studied in mainstream medicine. Some trials show symptom benefits in a number of areas, including those who suffer with asthma, high blood pressure, migraine headaches and childhood diabetes. Other research findings suggest that not only does touch lower stress levels, but it also can boost the immune system and slow or even halt the progress of disease.[2] The right foot of a statue in St. Peter's Square is just short of disappearing because so many people have bent over and kissed it. Kissing statues is one thing, touching real people is entirely another.

Marasmus is the medical term for the destructive force that infants encounter when they are not given sufficient touch. A small infant will die if the child does not receive the right amount of touch from its caregiver within the first few weeks of life outside the womb. This is true in every culture on every continent of the earth. People die for lack of touch. This hands-off mentality is not only killing our children, it's killing our employees in our companies as well. Too many people believe that touching is somehow taboo.

In Massachusetts, I heard there were those trying to draft a law that will make it a *crime* to sit on Santa's lap.[3] Touching is *essential* to life. According to an article in *HomeLife Magazine*, American parents touch their kids only two times per hour on average.[4] The essential power of touch reminds us that we are affectionately loved. It reminds us that someone is there. Is it any wonder that our culture is filling up with "touch" crimes today? If you touch too little, it will create monsters who touch too much. Jesus was a "touch" freak! He even touched lepers — those who were *"untouchable."*

When the space shuttle *Challenger* exploded in midair in 1986, seven crewmembers lost their lives. Disintegration of the entire vehicle began after an O-ring seal in its right solid rocket booster failed at liftoff. The crew compartment and many other shuttle fragments were eventually recovered from the ocean floor after a lengthy search and recovery operation. Although the exact timing of the death of the crew is unknown, several crewmembers are

---

2 "How the Power of Touch reduces pain and even fights disease" by: Roger Dobson, October 2006.
3 Someone needs their head examined.
4 *HomeLife*, September 1998, 66.

known to have survived the initial breakup of the spacecraft. However, the shuttle had no escape system and the astronauts did not survive the impact of the crew compartment with the ocean surface.

"The last words spoken on the Challenger came from one of the crew: *"Give me your hand."*

This was a scientific analysis, followed by a startling discovery. According to the *"official"* transcripts, a voice believed to be that of Michael J. Smith can be heard exclaiming *"uh-oh."* This was a telltale sign that the crew was clued in on their limited future. What follows is nothing short of amazing. The last words spoken on the Challenger came from one of the crew: *"Give me your hand."*[5] Out of everything that could have been done or spoken in those last few seconds, it all ended in a glorious moment of touch. Whether it was Ronald McNair, Dick Scobee, Michael Smith, Ellison Onizuka or Gregory Jarvis — one of them spoke the four finest words of the 20th century. He was most likely speaking to Christa McAuliffe or Judith Resnik. I don't care how educated you might be. I don't care how powerful you think you are or what kind of position you hold within your company or family. If you don't know when to take the hand of a person in need, I would surmise that you will never become the person you were created to be.

Have you hugged your children today? Your husband? Your wife? I think you know what to do.

Old Yeller Syndrome

Do you remember the words; *"Go on! Get outta' here you stupid ole yeller dog!"* Anyone familiar with the Disney film *Old Yeller*[6] will recall those heart-wrenching words. In a nutshell, the Coates family are settlers making their way in the Texas hill country during the late 19th century. While the father is away on a cattle drive to obtain money, an "old yeller dog" visits the family uninvited. Travis, the eldest son, tries to shoo the dog away, but his younger brother

5 Time Magazine; Dec. 24, 1990.
6 *Old Yeller* is a 1956 novel by Fred Gipson. The title is taken from the name of the fictional big yellow dog who is a main character in the book.

Arliss immediately takes to the stray dog. Their mother intervenes, reasoning that the family could use a good dog around the ranch. Though Travis initially loathes the "rascal," Old Yeller eventually proves his worth, saving Travis, Arliss and the family on several occasions. Travis grows to love Old Yeller.

The rightful owner of Yeller eventually shows up looking for his dog. After Arliss throws a fit, the owner recognizes that the family needs Yeller and so he trades him to Arliss in return for a home-cooked meal. By this time during the film you too are attached to the poor mutt. Unfortunately the story ends when Yeller becomes exposed to hydrophobia (rabies) after an encounter with a rabid wolf while defending the family. In order to prevent his beloved dog from further suffering, Arliss tearfully shoots the poor dog in order to speed his inevitable death.

Old Yeller Syndrome occurs when people who feel the need (right or wrong) to end a relationship suddenly turn on that person to the bewilderment of all involved. If one detects an inevitable ending of a relationship regardless of the reasons, they may become smug, nasty, insulting, and downright mean even though the relationship has many years of harmonious history. Those who increase don't do this sort of thing. They confront the issues head-on and take full responsibility for their actions in these situations. In other words, they don't throw stones before shooting the "dog."

It's disconcerting when Arliss calls the poor mutt "stupid" and "old" before actually killing the mad beast. He completely disregards the dog's heroism and undying love because he (Arliss) cannot bear the pain of losing Yeller. Arliss' lack of maturity becomes the undoing of the relationship emotionally before he ends the relationship physically.

After 25 years of marriage and raising three beautiful children, I have personally experienced among some of my relationships — including some of my own family members, how family can turn on family, father on mother, husband on wife, etc. What do we do with those who stab us in the back? This is where we really get to be who we say we are. Hate the actions, but love the person. Loving the person does not mean that we stay in situations with an abuser. It does mean that we work to a place of universal forgiveness, and when we are mad as hell, we let it out with those we trust.

God hears our cries. He will heal and restore us, whether in this life or the next. Abraham and the fathers of the faith received God's promise from a distance, and the world was not worthy of them! Always remember: Faith is believing what we cannot see. It is living our lives in the context that we are on our way to another place, where there is no disease, sickness or death — heaven with our Father, God.

Final Overview

In time, you will understand the power of *Accidental Increase* if you haven't begun the process already. It begins with character and ends with character. As I look back over these 25 years, I can see how these principles have worked in my own life and it feels accidental when I think of how they have moved me to where I now stand. I seemed to have taken on the DNA of all those who have had a part in my early and mid-life development. I am a sponge for principles and insights that make life easier and more fun.

We have looked at receiving vs. achieving and how ambition actually works against us. Allowing your destiny to chase you is far more productive than living the life of Johnny Quest.

Remember your ethos. Remember how others perceive you and determine your impact on their life. If you are seen as one of good will and intention, knowledgeable and caring, you will be given access to their heart.

Being ambitious about helping others get what they need always results in having your own needs met as well. Live out of the middle of your life and learn to recognize the voice of God within you. And once you have heard it, do what he says without argument.

Don't be a jerk! Allow yourself to be drafted into your life position. Stop comparing yourself with others. If everyone were an ear, how would we see? Embrace your weaknesses and capitalize on your strengths. Learn to fail in public. Understand that God is proud of you and build your wings on the way down for once. Wake up to the fact that ducks don't always come in rows.

Live! If you feel like a misfit, understand that you may not be suited for your environment right now. So change it! If you don't like your job, get another one. If you don't like your family, well you're screwed (just kidding).

Learn to work through your mountains and stop going around them. Take a look in the mirror with the understanding that it never lies. Own your ideas. And for God's sake, be real. Remember the wisdom of the skin horse; *"It doesn't happen all at once. You become. It takes a long time. That's why it doesn't happen often to people who break easily, or have sharp edges, or who have to be carefully kept. Generally, by the time you are Real, most of your hair has been loved off, and your eyes drop out and you get loose in the joints and very shabby. But these things don't matter at all, because once you are Real you can't be ugly, except to people who don't understand."*

To Reach Steve Sisler

steve@behavioralresourcegroup.com

www.accidentalincrease.com

Blog: http://stevesisler.wordpress.com